Pub V
on
The North York
Moors and Coast

Stephen Rickerby

Published by Sigma Leisure – an imprint of
Sigma Press, 1 South Oak Lane, Wilmslow, Cheshire SK9 6AR, England.

British Library Cataloguing in Publication Data
A CIP record for this book is available from the British Library.

ISBN: 1-85058-351-X

Typesetting and Design by: Sigma Press, Wilmslow, Cheshire.

Maps by: Manchester Free Press

Cover photograph: The Milburn Arms, Rosedale Abbey

Printed & bound by: Manchester Free Press, Longford Trading Estate, Thomas Street, Stretford, Manchester M32 0JT.   Tel: 061-864 4540

General Disclaimer

CONTENTS

Introduction

The Walks

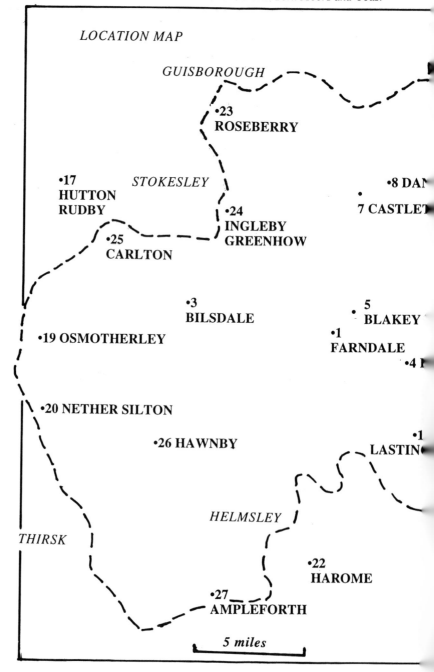

LOCATION MAP

GUISBOROUGH

•23
ROSEBERRY

•17
HUTTON
RUDBY

STOKESLEY

•8 DAN

7 CASTLET

•24
INGLEBY
GREENHOW

•25
CARLTON

•3
BILSDALE

5
BLAKEY

•19 OSMOTHERLEY

•1
FARNDALE

•4

•20 NETHER SILTON

•26 HAWNBY

•1
LASTIN

HELMSLEY

THIRSK

•22
HAROME

•27
AMPLEFORTH

5 miles

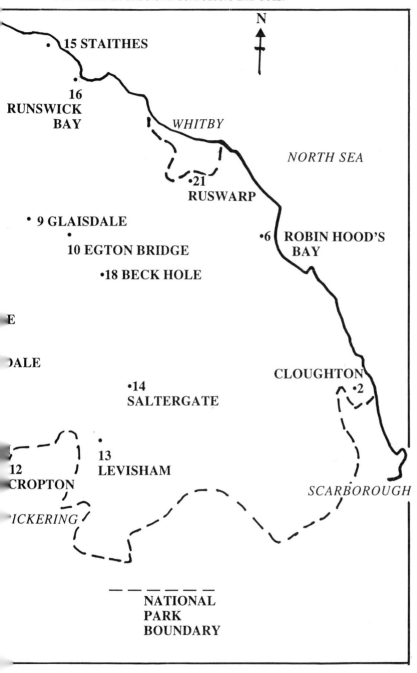

N

• **15 STAITHES**

**16
RUNSWICK
BAY**

WHITBY

NORTH SEA

•**21
RUSWARP**

• **9 GLAISDALE**

10 EGTON BRIDGE

•**18 BECK HOLE**

•6 **ROBIN HOOD'S
BAY**

E

)ALE

•**14
SALTERGATE**

CLOUGHTON
•2

**13
LEVISHAM**

**12
CROPTON**

ICKERING

SCARBOROUGH

**NATIONAL
PARK
BOUNDARY**

The North York Moors and Coast

The North York Moors form a plateau of heather moorlands reaching up to a thousand feet above sea-level and deeply dissected by lush green dales. They are surrounded by the Tees lowlands to the north, the Vales of Mowbray and Pickering to the west and south, and the beautiful and spectacular, if relatively little-known, Heritage Coast on the east.

The North York Moors National Park with its symbol, the 'Young Ralph' cross standing high on Blakey Ridge (Walk 5), covers over 550 square miles of coast and moorland, and nearly all the walks in this book lie within, or within sight of, its boundaries.

Geology and Scenery

The rocks underlying the Moors are mostly of relatively young Jurassic age (around 150 million years old) but are very varied and include shales and limestones, as well as gritstones and limestone. This geological variety is reflected in the scenery, for instance in the convoluted skyline of the Cleveland Hills where more resistant strata have allowed summits such as Roseberry Topping, capped by hard grit, to stand above the general level.

Dales dissect the plateau in a series, excepting the Esk, of mostly north-south trending incisions. But even the longest of these, Bilsdale, does not provide a completely through route from the Tees plain to the Vale of Pickering. Steep-sided Newton Dale (Walk 13) does stretch continuously from the south as far north as the Esk Valley. This is a relic of the Ice Age, eroded by meltwater spilling over from the lake which existed in Eskdale at that time and into another – Lake Pickering which flooded most of the present-day vale.

Another remnant of the Ice Age is the boulder clay to be found piled on much of the region's lower land, for instance in the Esk Valley and along the foot of the Cleveland Hills. This material of sticky clay embedded with stones was deposited by the ice as it melted at the close of the last Ice Age.

Along the coast is spectacular cliff scenery whose diversity is the result of a mixed geology of clays and shales, as well as the more resistant sandstones and limestone. The folded structure of the rock causes inlets to be eroded where rocks which are more susceptible to erosion come to the surface. This is the case at Robin Hood's Bay, for instance (Walk 6), and many of the softer cliffs are at risk from occasional landslips, as at Runswick (Walk 16) and Robin Hood's Bay again.

History and Settlement

The open heather moors are frequently and erroneously thought of as wilderness. In fact they are the product of human actions which began on the Moors in prehistoric times. Primitive hunters of animals and gatherers of berries are likely to have learned early to burn away upland trees to improve their hunting grounds.

North Yorkshire's first farmers came on the scene perhaps 5000 years ago and their monuments including burial mounds, or "howes" – as at Two Howes near Goathland (Walk 18), and stone circles – as at Studland Ring near Ampleforth (Walk 27) – remain a feature of the landscape today. So does the heather, for it is probably their cultivating and overgrazing of the uplands, coupled with climatic deterioration, which rendered the soil so acidic as to be unsuited to further farming, abandoning it to moor.

By the time of the Iron Age, about 2500 years ago, the dales were already settled and earthworks established to mark boundaries, for instance along the Hambleton Hills on the western edge of the plateau and above Bilsdale (Walk 3).

The Romans built forts and some roads, signal stations and camps, as at Cawthorn near Cropton. They did not establish settlements of any size in the Moors themselves, preferring, largely, to by-pass such a hostile and largely inaccessible region.

As for the works of the post-Roman Saxon and Norse invaders and colonists, many of today's place names date from these Dark Ages, including those ending in 'by' or 'dale' which are Norse and 'ham', 'ley' or 'ton' which are Anglo-Saxon. Viking words remain in today's language too – 'rigg' for ridge, 'beck' for stream and 'bramble' for blackberry, for example. At this time abbeys were founded at Whitby, where the Great Synod of 664 merged the Celtic and Roman churches, and at Lastingham (Walk 11).

In early Medieval times, the peasants of the Moors were subsistence farmers. Each parish contained land suitable for grazing, crops, timber and building stone so as to remain as self-sufficient as possible, although a good deal of trade by barter undoubtedly went on between them. Meanwhile, the monks of the great abbeys like Rievaulx established advanced and prosperous farms and a transport system of stone causeways, which partly remains today. Stone Crosses were built as markers, of which Young Ralph (Walk 5) is perhaps best known, and in the later Middle Ages pack horse bridges such as Duck Bridge near Danby (Walk 8). Beggar's Bridge between Glaisdale and Egton Bridge has its own tale to tell (see Walk 10).

During the centuries between the end of the Middle Ages and the beginning of the Industrial Revolution, larger areas of open land were enclosed in the dales and many of today's dry stone walls were built. Only the highest, least productive land remained as unfenced common pasture.

The Industrial Revolution had a greater effect on the Moors landscape than might at first meet the eye. Ironstone was mined in the Cleveland Hills, the Esk Valley and Rosedale and an elaborate transport system designed to take it to the furnaces of Middlesbrough to the north. Port Mulgrave's harbour was built (Walk 15), and so was the awe-inspiring railway from Rosedale over the moor tops (Walk 5) to the incline down the Cleveland Hills scarp at Ingleby Greenhow (Walk 24).

The settlement pattern which history has endowed to the twentieth century is one of market towns fringing the Moors: Pickering, Helmsley, Thirsk, Stokesley and Guisborough for example, and serving, at least in part, the villages and isolated farms of the interior dales. The villages themselves are mostly stone-built of sandstone in the north and west, Osmotherley for instance, and either honey-coloured limestone (as at Hutton-le-Hole) or the greyer limestone blocks of the south-eastern villages, including Cropton and Levisham.

Along the coast of course there are differences. Many of the villages there, like Staithes and Robin Hood's Bay were for centuries isolated communities of fishers and smugglers. They had little contact with the outside world until the coming of the railway and of motorised transport brought the influx of tourists including, of course, pub walkers!

The latter part of the twentieth century has seen the conservation of the landscape by the setting up of the National Park in 1952, to try to manage the environment left to us by nature and history, for the benefit of local and visitor alike.

Flora and Fauna of the Moors and Coast

The purple heather of the high moors is at its best in August to September. This is the archetypal floral image of the region, though in places it is at risk from bracken encroaching from the better-drained slopes where bilberry is also present. Other colourful plants include the white flowering cotton grass of wetter, peaty areas in late spring and the yellow bog asphodel to be spotted among the rushes.

Where native deciduous woods have survived, the species most commonly to be seen are sessile oak, birch, ash and alder, with bluebells and primroses sometimes among the ground cover. Willow, hazel, hawthorn and honeysuckle can also be seen, and, along hedgerows, brambles and sloes.

Birdlife is profuse on both moor and coast. Waders including golden plover, curlews, lapwings, and snipe are species to be seen on the coast in winter, and they also breed on the moors themselves. The Merlin, Britain's smallest bird of prey, is a creature of the heather, as are pipits, skylarks and human-encouraged game species, notably grouse and pheasant. Owls, especially in the woods, and, more occasionally buzzards, may also be expected.

Along the coast are fulmar, cormorants, gulls and kittiwakes and, in wooded areas, woodpeckers, wrens, warblers and fly-catchers, as well as woodcock and blackcap. Herons may also be observed in Spring.

Of the larger animals, shrews, foxes and hare are found on the open moors, as are adders (see Walk 20) and lizards. Badgers, mice, voles and squirrels are common in the woods. Rabbits, of course, are regularly to be seen and deer a little less so, mostly in the human-created forests of the southern North York Moors. Seals may sometimes be spotted along the shore.

Tradition and Folklore

Hobs of two types are central to the tradition and folklore of the North York Moors and Coast.

First, they are the pegs around which the quoit players of the region hope their heavy metal rings will land after being thrown the eleven yards from one clay bed to another. The game is known to have origins dating from at least the 14th century and is still played between pubs today, notably in the Esk Valley. Old photographs of quoit teams of the past adorn the walls of the Birch Hall Inn in Beck Hole (Walk 18) – a village where the game survives, as is Goldsborough on the coast (Walk 16).

Secondly, hobs are goblins, a sort of Yorkshire troll, who do good deeds and help out the humans whom they otherwise assiduously avoid. Glaisdale (see Walk 9) and Farndale (Walk 1) had their hobs, as did Hawnby, Egton, and Studford near Ampleforth – all locations in this book. Walk 12 takes you through Hob Hill Wood between Cropton and

Sinnington. The Farndale legend concerns Bob O'Hurst, a hob who, for generations, helped out a farming family in exchange for morning cream. Being short-changed by one of the latter generations, who tried to substitute mere skimmed milk for the cream, he took to causing mayhem instead. So much so that the family decided to give up and flee. However, the hob came too, so that they ended up staying on the farm – hob and all.

Shows are a part of the traditional country scene, and a village show in summer is a special delight. Places in this book with showdays you could visit as part of your pub walk include Osmotherley, Egton Gooseberry Show, Hinderwell (Walk 15), Danby, Rosedale, Bilsdale and Farndale – all in August, and Castleton in mid-September. For details of dates, ring one of the area's tourist information centres or the Moors Centre itself on 0287 660654.

Legends of smuggling are associated with the Saltersgate Inn (Walk 14) and the Dolphin Hotel in Robin Hood's Bay (walk 6) where customs officials reportedly surprised a gang with their contraband brandy. Obliged to sample the goods, the officers found it too much to their liking and, consequently, the smugglers made good their escape.

The Cleveland Way – and other paths

This National Trail stretches 108 miles around the fringe of the National Park from Helmsley to the Cleveland Hills themselves, and south again along the coast as far as Filey. Several of the walks here include a section of the Cleveland Way, recognisable by the distinctive acorn symbol on waymarkers.

The Cleveland Way is a horseshoe shape; there is a now no-longer missing link along the southern edge of the Moors, and as part of the Cropton walk (Walk 12), you will find yourself following the "Link" waymarkers for a time.

Both the famous Lyke Wake Walk and the national Coast to Coast walk also use the 12 mile stretch of the Way across the Cleveland Hills.

The Esk Valley Walk, part of which leads through Arncliffe Wood between Glaisdale and Egton Bridge (Walk 10), is a more recent regional long-distant path. It is 30 miles from Blakey Ridge to Whitby, and so the dolphin symbol is a suitable motivator for those attempting it.

Further to the south, those walking the route round Harome (Walk 22) can sample a short stretch of the Ebor Way.

Pubs and Ales

Pubs in this book have been chosen for themselves as well as the base for an interesting and hopefully enjoyable circular walk. This is a pub walks book, so both elements need equal consideration.

The pubs here are all real ale establishments with a friendly welcome and enjoyable atmosphere. They are also very different from each other in other ways. There are walkers' pubs (the Saltersgate Inn, for instance), friendly village locals (the White Horse at Ampleforth and Kings Head at Hutton Rudby, for example) and places with a little more up-market finesse such as the bar of the Hawnby Hotel. Most serve food and this too varies from sandwiches and bar fare to a la carte restaurant meals, occasionally with an exotic twist, as at the Blackwell Ox in Carlton.

Ales which are real are available in all these establishments. Many are brewed in the Yorkshire region, Theakstons at Masham, of course, but Cropton beer is brewed in the village for the New Inn itself – that really is local ale.

Despite recent legislation, pub opening hours remain a cat's cradle of complexity. Those given here are as given to me by the licensees. But if you are planning a walk which is likely to involve you calling at a pub outside conventional hours you would be well advised to telephone to check – telephone numbers are given for all pubs.

Public Transport

Getting to the pubs and home again is an important consideration for the pub walker. Access details are given for each establishment and most are accessible by public transport. Telephone numbers are given for local transport operators, but some regional points of contact you may need are: British Rail, Middlesbrough (0642 225535) and York (0904 642155), North York Moors Railway (0751 73535), Tees and District Buses (0947 602146, Whitby and 0642 210131, Middlesbrough) and Yorkshire Coastliner (0653 692556).

Details of all public transport services are given in a leaflet called Moors Connections and published by Elmtree Press, The Elms, Exelby, Bedale, North Yorkshire DL8 2HD. It is available from them for just the cost of postage and packing and is an invaluable guide for those intending to undertake several bus and train journeys.

Moorsbus services operate on Sundays and Bank Holidays from Spring to the end of summer and are a useful addition to the network for reaching some remoter spots from well outside the region. Services operate from Darlington, Stockton, Middlesbrough, Hull, Beverley and York. Contact Tees or Yorkshire Coastliner for exact details.

Both the British Rail operated Whitby to Middlesbrough Esk Valley Line and the privately-run North York Moors Railway are important access routes for the pub walker. The two interconnect at Grosmont.

The Walks

Walks in this book have been chosen to give you a taste of as many types of scenery as possible. There are walks on the high moors, along the coast, in the dales and on the surrounding lowlands with views of the hills from the vantage point of a lower altitude.

Some walks may be combined in pairs for a longer foray into the countryside, but please remember not to count on a rate in excess of two miles an hour if you are going to enjoy the scenery. Also, allow for the climbs inevitable in at least some walks in this upland region.

Appropriate pairs, properly planned, are:

❑ Walks 4 and 5 (Rosedale and Blakey Ridge)

❑ Walks 9 and 10 (Glaisdale and Egton Bridge)

❑ Walks 13 and 14 (Levisham and Saltergate)

❑ Walks 15 and 16 (Staithes and Runswick Bay)

❑ Walks 19 and 20 (Osmotherley and Nether Silton)

Map references are given using the two Ordnance Survey Outdoor Leisure Maps (1:25000 or 4cm to 1km) which completely cover the National Park and all the walks in this book. They are readily available and specially designed for the recreational user. For simplicity, grid references are kept to the six figures allowed by the grids on these maps: Sheets 26 and 27, North York Moors Western and Eastern areas respectively.

All the walks make use of public paths and by-ways. These should not be obstructed and were all passable when surveyed for this book. If you find a right of way obstructed, this is illegal, and you should complain to the County Council. Please use common sense on the day, however, and be prepared to make a detour in the final resort.

Land in the National Park is not owned by the nation. It belongs to private landowners – mostly the farmers. Keep to the paths, keep dogs on leads, use gates and leave them as you find them, avoid noise, litter and fire. Be prepared properly in the interest of your own safety and that of others – stout footwear and waterproofs are essential on the high moors.

Happy Walking!

Walk 1: Farndale

Route: Church Houses – Low Blakey Moor – Oak Cragg – Cragg Cottage – Low Mill – High Mill ("The Daffodil Walk") – Church Houses

Distance: $5^1/_4$ miles

Map: O.S. Outdoor Leisure 26, North York Moors Western Area (SW Sheet)

Start: Feversham Arms, Church Houses (Grid reference 669975)

Access: Church Houses is a hamlet in the northern part of Farndale, 6 miles north of Hutton-le-Hole, off the Blakey Road to Westerdale. From the north it is accessible by car by turning right at the Lion Inn on Blakey Ridge.

The Feversham Arms (0751 33206)

A traditional country inn, stone built, with a flagstoned floor and cast iron range, the Feversham Arms (Lord and Lady Feversham live at Duncombe Park, Helmsley – a stately home open to the public) serves Tetley Bitter as its real ale. There are bar meals lunchtime and evening and the restaurant opens in the evening, although bookings are advised. On Sundays there is a traditional Yorkshire Sunday lunch. Opening times are 11am to 2.30pm and 6 to 11pm in summer and in winter (from mid-September) 12 to 2.30pm and 7 to 10.30pm. The outside beer garden really does have a lovely dale setting.

Farndale

Settlement in Farndale is dispersed along the dale, with just two clustered hamlets at Church Houses, which has the pub, and Low Mill, which has the Post Office. Between the two wend the two miles of the Daffodil Walk for which the dale is most renowned. The golden host is usually best seen in the second-half of April, but the wander along the east bank of the River Dove makes a lovely ending to this circular walk at any time of year.

The Feversham Arms

Farndale Show is a fascinating occasion – a really authentic country show held at Church Houses on August Bank Holiday Monday.

The Walk

With your back to the front door of the Feversham Arms, turn right along the road and walk up the lane in the direction which is signposted to Hutton-le-Hole as far as the junction. Initially, you follow the road to the right (signposted to Hutton-le-Hole again and to Gillamoor).

Having turned right, you will come across two public footpath signs pointing uphill. Choose the rightward bearing path and head up the

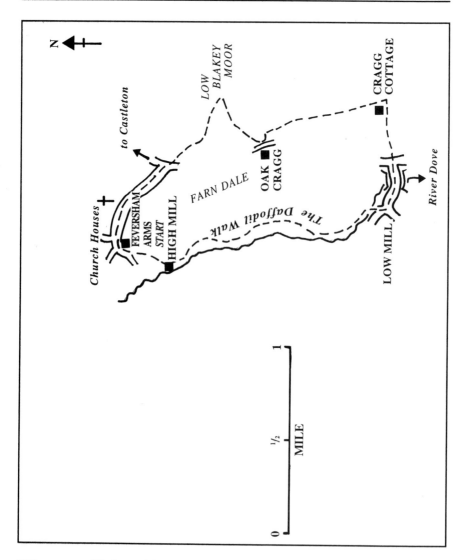

little, grassy V-shaped lane to a stile leading to a gulley. The path leads along the right of this gulley to a gap in the dry stone wall ahead.

Beyond the gap, a wooden stile takes you over a fence. Keep to the right of the gulley with the fence and dry stone wall field boundary on your right. Hugging this field boundary initially, you will find the path heading uphill to the left towards a rock outcrop as this becomes visible.

The path curves gently leftward around the rock outcrop through a clearly defined small gap before flattening out. Carry straight ahead here toward an isolated boulder directly in line with the path. From here you can see a dry stone wall ahead, crossed by a stile just to the left. Head for this stile.

Cross the stile, which is at the meeting point of three dry stone walls. Turn right and follow the dry stone wall to a right angle corner. At this corner, turn right and follow the wall down to a wooden gate. Passing through the gate, follow the track round to the left and then the right. Walking down this now stony track, the buildings of Oak Cragg become visible directly ahead.

A few yards above a dry stone wall, the track divides into three. Take the centre track. Proceed straight ahead and on through a gate into a gulley and down along this to the minor road at Oak Cragg. Turn left along the road.

Immediately visible is the waymarked footpath to follow to the left. Cross this stile and walk straight ahead to the stream crossed by a small unwalled stone bridge leading to a waymarked stile over a dry stone wall. Over the stile, walk across the field along the bottom of the wooded bankside, crossing a water course and possibly a temporary wire stock control into the next pasture. Follow the path, keeping the dry stone wall on your left.

Look out for the next stile which is three trees along the opposite field boundary. Crossing this stile, make for the next, which is directly across the field, but you should walk round the edge of the field to reach it. Cross this last wooden stile and follow the path ahead to a gate and footpath signpost. Press on for a few yards, possibly through quite high ferns in summer, to a stone stile. Carry on with the dry stone wall of the enclosed pastures on your right until you cross a second stone stile after passing Cragg House a field away to the right.

Joining the track next to Cragg Cottage, bearing a little rightward, and keeping the dry stone wall on your right, you head slightly downhill towards a wooden gate. Pass through this gate and a second a little further down the slope.

Walk down the track downhill and through a third gate down to the minor road junction. Cross the road and follow the signpost towards Low Mill and Gillamoor into Farndale Nature Reserve.

At Low Mill you arrive at another minor road junction where you should turn right past the chapel. Go up to the small car park opposite the Post Office where the path to High Mill is clearly signposted through a gate.

Follow the flagstoned path down to a second gate by the stream. Cross the wooden footbridge here and turn left through the single wooden gate. Cross a second stream by means of a footbridge and pass through the ensuing kissing gate. Follow the now obvious path ahead across the fields, parallel to the River Dove to your left.

Along the way you will pass through a wooden gap stile and find a wooden handrail to guide you down to a duckboard bridge across to the next pasture. The stream meanders here. Beyond the river loop the path divides and you need to take the right fork to another keyhole type stile.

Carry straight on along the obvious path alongside the river until you emerge from a wooded section via a kissing gate on which there are waymark arrows for straight ahead and right. Take the straight ahead option and walk across the field to a small stone bridge.

Arriving at High Mill, follow the track between the stone buildings, and you will soon see Church Houses ahead.

Walk 2: Cloughton

Route: Blacksmiths Arms – Cloughton Station – Cloughton Wyke – Hayburn Wyke – Dismantled Railway Path – Court Green Farm – Cloughton

Distance: $5^1/4$ miles

Map: O.S. Outdoor Leisure 27, North York Moors Eastern Area (SE Sheet)

Start: The Blacksmith's Arms (Grid reference 008944)

Access: Cloughton lies on the A171 Scarborough to Whitby road 5 miles north of Scarborough. You can reach it by bus using the Scarborough Skipper service 15 (0723 375463) from Monday to Saturday and Botterill's (0751 74210) locally-operated bus on Thursday and Saturday only. Tees Bus service 93 from Middlesbrough, Whitby and Scarborough calls at Cloughton seven days a week.

The Blacksmiths Arms (0723 870244)

A stone-built pub still sited next to the working village blacksmith's shop. Inside is a bar at the rear, leading directly off the car park, and a front lounge with beams and a real fire. Bar meals are served lunchtimes and evenings and there is also a separate restaurant with à la carte menu. Opening hours are 11.30am to 2pm and 6.30 to 11pm and the hand-pulled ale on offer is Worthington Best Bitter.

Cloughton

Cloughton is a pleasant village with some lovely stone cottages sited firmly astride the main Whitby to Scarborough road, but just inland from one of the quietest, most attractive stretches of coast. Formerly on the Whitby to Scarborough railway, dismantled in the early 1960s, the village would have had some commuter traffic into and out of

Scarborough, and the twentieth century houses of Station Lane perhaps reflect that.

The Blacksmith's Arms

Hayburn Wyke

A wyke is an inlet of the sea, and Hayburn Wyke is one of the prettiest and most interesting along the Heritage Coast of Cleveland and North Yorkshire. It is a secluded, wooded valley and wild life reserve cut into the gritstone rock as Hayburn Beck cascades to the sea over a series of waterfalls, the last of which, unusually, falls directly onto the beach.

The beach is a rocky one, covered by smoothly rounded boulders – the result of the erosive action of the sea as waves throw them against each other and the shore.

In Victorian days railway excursions from York and Scarborough brought visitors to Hayburn Wyke to enjoy the woods and tea at the hotel which was built next to the station on the cliff top.

The Walk

Facing the Blacksmiths Arms from the opposite side of the road, head off right, along the street and down to turn left between the houses of Station Lane. Just past the end of speed limit road signs, turn left onto the old railway path, through a gate. This is opposite Station House – the old railway station whose platform is still quite evident.

Simply carry on along the line of the dismantled former Whitby to Scarborough railway, until you pass under a stone bridge. Turn immediately left, up a set of waymarked steps. At the top, pass through the gate on your left and then turn left onto the lane, over the bridge and towards the sea.

Pass through a metal gate as you continue along the lane towards the sea, ignoring a signposted public footpath to your right. At the end of the lane is a wooden bench which overlooks the rocky inlet of Cloughton Wyke. Follow the Cleveland Way to the left of the inlet and up onto the cliff top.

Keep going along the Cleveland Way as it wends its way up and down the cliff-line and enjoy the coastal scenery along the way. Looking back from high points you can see, on a clear day, beyond Scarborough Castle, as far as Flamborough Head.

Above Hayburn Wyke, the path dips down across a waymarked stile into woodland. Follow the path down through the trees to a waymark sign where you turn right, although just to your left is a National Trust information table which you may care to study first.

Follow the path down towards the shore, around a series of bends as it descends the steep valley side, turning right at a second waymark sign and passing a footbridge on your left before finally reaching the beach itself.

From the beach, begin by setting off back along the path which led you down to the waterfall, passing the footbridge on your right this time and coming back to the Cleveland Way sign. Follow the yellow waymark arrow straight ahead, glimpsing another waterfall through the trees on your right, and up, though a wooded glade, to a crossing of the ways.

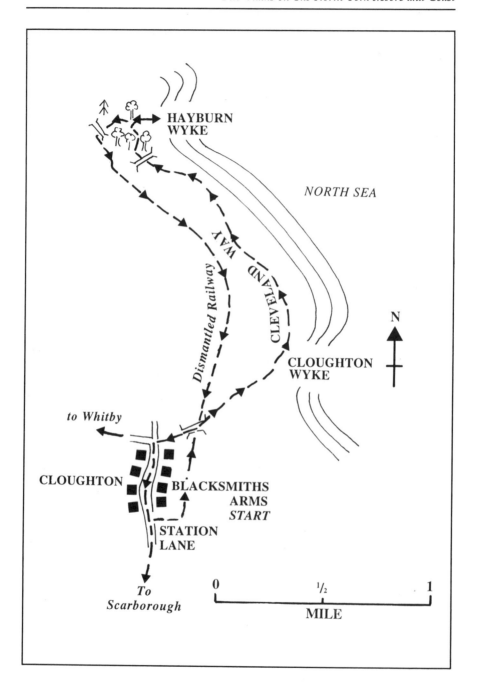

Carry straight on until the path brings you to a track at a T-junction. Turn right and across the waymarked stile, bearing left along the track, through the pasture. Follow the track as it curves left to a further stile. Cross this and carry on past the remains of the old railway station, following the lane up and around to the right.

By a large concrete gatepost, turn left through the gate onto the old railway path. Carry on the railway until you come to the bridge over the track where you left it earlier. Climb the same set of steps to the gate on your left, but this time turn right, along the lane, to Cloughton.

Coming to the top of Newlands Lane, turn left to walk down the village's main street to the Blacksmith's Arms.

Hayburn Wyke

Walk 3: Bilsdale

Route: Chop Gate – William Beck Farm – Medd Crag – Round Hill – Carr Ridge – Urra – Bilsdale Hall – Chop Gate

Distance: $9^3/_4$ miles

Map: O.S. Outdoor Leisure 26, North York Moors Western Area (SW and NW Sheets)

Start: Buck Inn, Chop Gate (Grid reference 559997)

Access: Chop Gate is on the B1257 road, 7 miles south of Stokesley. By bus, it is accessible by Tees bus service 294 from Stokesley and Helmsley.

The Buck Inn (0642 778334)

Dating from the 1750s, the Buck Inn at Chop Gate (locally, "Chopyatt") offers food each lunchtime and evening, ranging from sandwiches and bar meals, to the restaurant's à la carte menu. Sunday lunches are served. Opening hours are 11.30am to 3pm and 6pm to 11.30pm (7pm opening in winter). There is a beer garden with children's play equipment outside. Beers available include Vaux Samson and Lorimers Bitter.

Bilsdale

Bilsdale is one of the main dales of the North York Moors and provides the natural route corridor south from Stokesley to Helmsley. Settlement is dispersed along the dale, and there is no single, nucleated village.

Chop Gate is perhaps the largest habitation, with the Buck Inn pub, primary school and small church as services to offer the local population.

The Buck Inn

"Cromwell's Trenches"

Ancient earthworks rim the western slope of Urra Moor and are followed by two sections of this walk. Whatever their origin, these are considerably older than Civil War vintage. They probably represent an Iron Age land boundary, rather than a defensive fortification, despite their imposing outlook over the dale.

The Walk

From the Buck Inn, head south (turning right if you are walking out of the front door) alongside the road, past the village car park, and Esp House on the left, ignoring the unmarked stile into the field. Carry on alongside the road until a track, signposted for Bransdale, leads left. Follow this track straight along to William Beck Farm, the initial wire fence on your left reverting to dry stone wall *en route*.

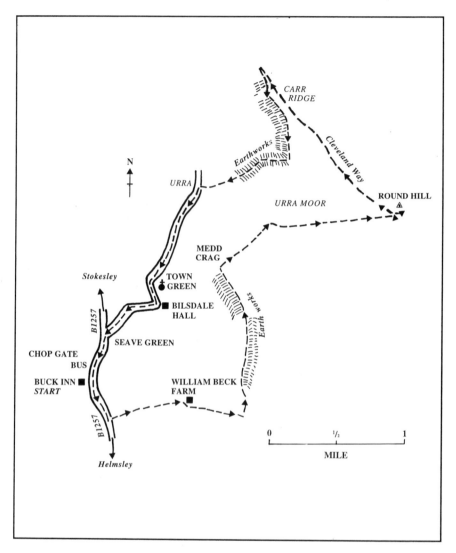

At William Beck Farm, the track bends right, across the front of the farmhouse, and then, initially, left, round the side and through a gateway. Then head right, away from the gravel track, following the waymarker across grass.

Arriving at a gate, pass through and straight ahead, negotiating a small sheep hurdle gate, as you follow the trodden path alongside a gulley and between two dry stone walls. A gate leads you onto a grass path and past a spring on your left, before bringing you to a second gate and thence on to more open moorland – Black Intake. Crossing this enclosure you reach a further gate, set in a dry stone wall, and taking you onto heather moor.

Continue straight ahead to a track crossing your path. Turn left onto this track, which is a diversion of the rights of way as they appear on the O.S. map, and follow it to a junction where three tracks meet. Turn left onto the track that leads downhill to the corner of a dry stone wall and then follow the track around to the right and the ancient earthworks are soon evident on your right.

Continue past East Bank Plantation on your left and on until the track bends right and passes through the earthworks. At this point, take the grass path to the left, parallel to the trend of the dale and alongside the earthwork which is now on your left.

Follow the path downhill and then parallel to the dry stone wall a few yards over to your left. Reaching the far corner of this wall, carry straight ahead along the line of the earthwork until you cross a water course. You arrive at a crossing of tracks where, on turning right, you see a large wooden notice exhorting visitors to care for the landscape. Walk past this notice and up the hillside.

Reaching a corner where three tracks join, you will find a wooden sign pointing to Bloworth Crossing. Continue straight ahead along the track towards Bloworth Crossing, passing grouse butts on your left numbered 9 to 1, and on across the heather Urra Moor, taking in extensive views in all directions.

As a second track, from North Gill Head, joins your route, the triangulation pillar on Round Hill is visible directly ahead. Round Hill, at 454m, is the highest point on the North York Moors. Passing a cairn on your left, you arrive at a T-junction of pathways where a stone marker is engraved A. M. Beside it, a sign, on which is hand-painted "Blow" and a direction arrow leading you rightward. The triangulation pillar is now ahead of you, but diagonally across to your left.

Following the track, you will pass the triangulation pillar over to your left and come across a boundary stone on your left. Turn left at this stone and follow the path through the heather to the triangulation pillar itself. From the triangulation pillar, the trodden path leads you down to a pile of stones and then straight on and down through the heather onto the Cleveland Way, turning right as you join it.

Follow the Cleveland Way, without the necessity to make any directional decisions, onto Carr Ridge, passing a series of cairns en route. Eventually, a dry stone wall becomes evident several yards over to your right on the hill brow and approaches the track ever more closely until you can see where it meets it at a gate.

As you near the gate, turn left onto the bridleway which follows the top of the earthwork until after crossing a water course, you arrive at a dividing of the ways where you should turn right and head downward.

Reaching a larger stream, cross it, and clamber up onto the continued path on the other side. This is the stream close to Cowkill Well (581024) which is marked on the O.S. 1:25 000 map. The path continues to follow the earthworks.

On reaching a gulley, turn right to follow the straight path at its base until the buildings of Urra Farm become visible ahead. Here the path branches slightly left and takes you alongside the gulley before bending left beside three tabular boulders.

A dry stone wall is now on your right, which then becomes a wire fence. Follow them until you come to a waymarked gate. Turn right, through this gate, and down the gulley in front of you to the gate in the field corner. Turn left, alongside the minor road, at Urra and follow it past Maltkiln House on your right and down to St Hilda's church at Town Green. Carry on down the road to Bilsdale Hall where there is a sharp right-hand bend taking you down to the T-junction with the B1257 at Seave Green.

Turn left along it until you arrive back at the Buck Inn.

Walk 4: Rosedale

Route: Rosedale Abbey – North Dale – Knottside Plantation – Hill Cottages – Bell End – River Seven – Rosedale Abbey

Distance: $4^1/_2$ miles

Map: O.S. Outdoor Leisure 26, North York Moors Western Area (SW Sheet)

Start: The Milburn Arms (Grid reference 725959)

Access: Rosedale Abbey village is accessible from the north via minor road from Castleton (10 miles) or Danby (9 miles) and from the south by means of the road from Hutton-le-Hole (5 miles) and other villages such as Wrelton along the A170 Helmsley to Pickering road. The locally operated, once weekly Lockers Coaches (0751 73000) bus service is of little value to the day visitor. It is primarily intended to take locals to Pickering market on Mondays, departing Rosedale early morning and returning from Pickering at lunchtime.

The Milburn Arms (07515 312)

This stone-built 15th century inn is a Grade 2 listed building and has an attractive garden setting in the picturesque valley of Rosedale. Real ales are Theakstons (Bitter, XB and Old Peculier), Stones and Bass. The Milburn Arms has been a northern regional finalist in the "Pub Cook of the Year" competition in both 1991 and 1992 and serves bar meals and sandwiches in the bar, as well as a daily changing menu in its Priory Restaurant. There are picnic tables in the garden. Opening hours are 11.30am to 3.30pm and 6.30 to 11pm weekdays, and 12 to 3pm and 7 to 10.30pm on Sundays. Accommodation, including en-suite, is also available. This pub is shown on the cover.

Rosedale Abbey

Rosedale Abbey is the main settlement of Rosedale and lies right at the heart of the National Park. Almost nothing remains of the 12th Century Cistercian nunnery (founded in 1158 and dissolved in 1535) after which the village is named – only a ruined tower close by the church.

A century ago Rosedale was a busy mining valley, whose ironstone was taken by train over the high moors and down the incline at Ingleby Greenhow to the steelworks of Middlesbrough. Iron miners' cottages are still to be seen – including Hill Cottages which you will pass on this walk.

North Dale, Rosedale

The Walk

From the Milburn Arms front door, turn left and left again through the car park to a single wooden gate. Pass through this and onto the public footpath which leads across the field to a stile in the far left corner.

Over the stile into a pasture field, the grass path leads you straight across the middle to a stile and over on to a clear path. Beyond this, it skirts the edge of the subsequent field, stream and trees on your left. Follow the stream and pass through a gap in a dry stone wall and into a further pasture. The path clearly veers right, away from the stream and to a gap in the dry stone wall on the other side of the field.

The path now rejoins the stream and brings you to another gap in a dry stone wall, with adjacent stile. Continue across the next pasture which brings you in turn to a stile with an apparent choice of two waymarked routes, to right and left.

Cross the little stone bridge over the water course and go into the next pasture. The clear grass path takes you along the bottom of the slope, stream to the left, to a ladder stile over the far field boundary – a dry stone wall.

Having crossed the stile, you follow the path as it bends upward to the right along the bank of the stream. A second and waymarked ladder stile is reached at the junction of two dry stone walls. From the top of the stile you can see a gateway about 45 degrees over to your right to which the path leads.

Pass through this gateway and head for the single wooden gateway between trees. This is directly opposite, though not visible until you are about halfway across this undulating field.

Beyond this single gateway, a bridge of half a dozen stones takes you across a water course into the next pasture, where the way divides. Turn left and hug the field boundary on your left as far as the corner of the field. Here there is quite a steep drop down to the river, which you do not go down. Instead turn right and follow along the edge of the pasture until you are about halfway across the field where the path leads down the bank at an angle and to a gate.

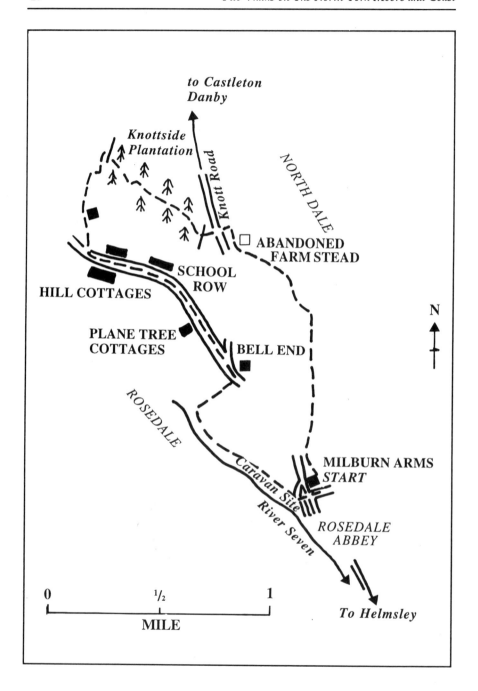

Passing through the gate, you arrive at a wooden footbridge which you cross, over North Dale Beck, emerging through a single wooden gate. A choice of routes presents itself. Follow the signposted bridleway straight ahead through the leftward of two gaps in the dry stone wall opposite.

Proceed with dry stone wall on your right and a steep bank to your left. At the next field boundary, pass through a gap in the dry stone wall, carrying on, straight ahead. Having now risen a few feet in altitude, you will find quite a steep drop down to the river to your right and a sloping pasture to your left.

At the field corner are two green signs and a surfaced farm track. Veer left to the second sign post which directs you along the footpath through a gap in the dry stone wall. Head across the pasture, along its right-hand edge, until you reach a wooden ladder stile.

Cross the stile, and follow the path as it heads off leftward, obliquely up and across the field towards a single tree. To the left of this tree, the path passes through a gate space in the dry stone wall. Continue along the clear path as it crosses an area of rougher pasture and dips down and up to cross a small water course. At the top of the little rise up from this water course, there is a parting of the ways.

Take the left-hand path, which does not appear to be the widest. Pass through some reeds and up toward a substantial single tree where there is a wire fence. From the corner of the fence the path becomes more clearly trodden as you follow the fence on your right. Over the fence is a pond and an abandoned farmstead.

Beyond the farmstead, the path leads you up to a gate in the corner of an area of woodland. Turn left here and follow the track you find, uphill a little, towards the minor road, though bending slightly left just before you reach it via a gate where there is a public right of way sign.

The Knott Road lies almost on the watershed. Behind you is North Dale, and ahead is Rosedale itself. Turn right along the road to the public footpath sign you can see ahead of you. At the sign, cross the waymarked stile and turn right along the fence line.

Almost immediately, the path leads you down to a waymark post with two alternative directions – straight ahead and left. Take the straight ahead option through the coniferous plantation. Coming to a waymarked stile, cross over and continue straight ahead through the trees, along a grass path and passing a straight ahead waymarker.

There is much more planting here than may be marked on your O.S. map. Keep following the path until you emerge at the plantation edge and onto a bridleway heading down leftward to reach a farmstead (Grid reference 707978).

Follow the track through the farmyard until it joins the minor road at Hill Cottages. Turn left between the cottages and follow the road past School Row and Plane Tree Cottages to the junction where you carry straight on as far as the holiday cottages at Bell End. Here, at the right angled bend, take the signposted public footpath off to the right, through a wooden gate and into a pasture.

Cross the pasture field, hedge to your left, and cross the stile into woodland. Follow the waymarked path down among brambles and then veering left to the River Seven. Turn left and, keeping the river on your right, ignore a couple of footbridges and come to a stile which you cross into a pasture field. The waymarked path then takes you along the left-hand edge of the field, rises up an embankment, and along the right-hand edge of the subsequent field, alongside the hedgerow.

Arriving at a stile, continue along the right-hand edge of the field until a caravan site is reached on your right. Carry straight on through the kissing gate and follow the caravan site driveway into Rosedale Abbey.

Passing the caravan site recreation field on your right, you will find that the driveway curves right. At this bend, turn left across the grass behind a stone cottage towards a dry stone wall.

The dry stone wall is crossed by means of a stone stile, and you find yourself in the streets of the village. Turn right and, passing the church on your left, take a left down the alley between a stone building to the right and the hedge leading to the remains of the stone tower. This is the last vestige of the Cistercian Nunnery.

Passing through an iron gate, veer right and walk along the front of the row of stone-built cottages to a second iron gate leading you out onto the street. The Milburn Arms is now visible over to your left.

Walk 5: Blakey Ridge

Route: The Lion Inn – Dale Head Farm – Sturdy Bank – George Gap Causeway – White Cross – The Lion Inn

Distance: 6 miles

Map: O.S. Outdoor Leisure 26, North York Moors Western Area (NW and SW Sheets)

Start: The Lion Inn (Grid reference 679997 – SW sheet)

Access: The Lion Inn is beside the road which runs the length of Blakey Ridge, from Castleton 5 miles to the north, to Hutton-le-Hole seven miles to the south.

The Lion Inn (075 15 320)

The Lion Inn is the moor top pub par excellence. It is sited on the top of Blakey Ridge, just $1^1/_2$ miles south of Young Ralph cross – the North York Moors National Park symbol, on the top of a truly blasted heath. Stories abound of customers cut off in the depth of the winter snows and young bloods are reputed to drive up from Teesside in the express hope of being stranded in the pub.

Its thick walls are undoubtedly necessary, but inside it is warm and welcoming with real fires and cosy decor. Certainly it has been refurbished and enlarged, but this has been done tastefully and is appropriate for the volume of its clientele – numbers, rather than size – especially in summer.

The Lion is open "all day, every day" which means from 10.30am to 11pm. and serves appropriately substantial bar meals from 11am to 10pm seven days a week. There is a separate dining room as well as the three sitting areas. There is an outer bench and an internal porch, more an air lock really, for people to remove muddy boots.

The fourth-highest pub in England, in terms of altitude above sea level, serves Tetley Bitter, Youngers No. 3 and Theakstons Best Bitter, XB and Old Peculier. It dates from the 15th century and offers fantastic views over the moors from its beer garden – in season.

The highest pub in England, for the record, is the Tan Hill Inn in the North Pennines, on the Yorkshire-Durham border.

Blakey Ridge

A long and narrow stretch of upland, Blakey Ridge separates Farndale to the west from Rosedale to the east and provides the foundation for some of the North York Moors famous stone crosses. Apart from Young Ralph itself, which stands beside the road at the crossroads from Hutton-le-Hole, Westerdale, Castleton and Rosedale, medieval Old Ralph stands close by. And the White Cross, nicknamed Fat Betty, is less than half a mile down the Rosedale road.

The legendary explanation for these stones, and the nearby Margery Stone, is that Ralph, an old servant from Rosedale nunnery escorted Sister Elizabeth (Betty) to Blakey Ridge to meet Sister Margery from another priory. The pair was lost in fog which descended. They sat down to wait for it to clear and so were able to meet Sister Margery as intended. Old Ralph erected the crosses to mark the occasion.

It is certainly the case that coins were traditionally placed on Young Ralph and beneath the top stone of the White Cross by travellers with money for the benefit of their poorer fellows who might happen along later.

The Walk

From the Lion Inn, cross the road and turn right alongside it until you come to a public footpath indicator pointing you leftward across the moor. Follow this along, with a wire fence on your left, through the heather to the bottom corner of the enclosure.

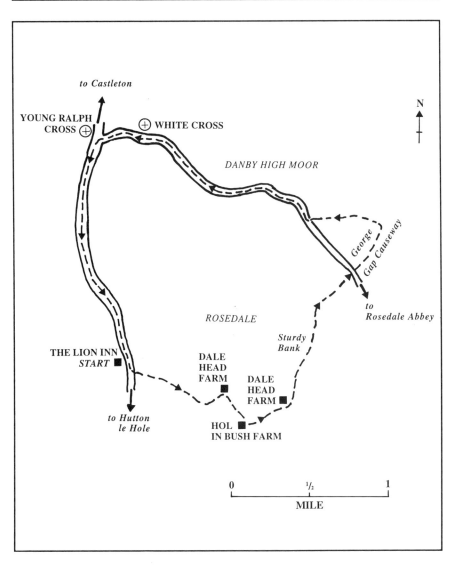

Carry straight on to the line of the old railway which virtually encircled Rosedale. Turn right along the dismantled railway and walk along the track until you come to a low cairn on your left. The path follows a line of cairns, of which this is the first.

So, turn left and follow the path from the first to second cairns, through the heather. By the time you have reached the second cairn, the path is evident as a green strip through the heather. Follow it down and across the dale-side to a pair of further low cairns. From the second of these you can see the path as a grassy strip through the heather.

Follow the path to a fifth low cairn. From here the grassy strip of the path is again evident as it enters a gulley to dip down to the left. Half-way round the gulley you can see, ahead and below, the buildings of Dale Head Farm.

Emerging from the gulley at a grouse butt numbered 7, you continue along the path as it curves right between two banks, initially. Keep following the trodden path until you reach a track at a noticeable bend. The path crosses this track and heads straight on as a green strip. Follow it down and, through another gulley, back onto the farm track at another bend.

Follow the bend down for a few yards and then leave it to follow the green strip of the path which continues straight ahead, directly towards Dale Head Farm. At the farm, pass through the gate into the yard. Walk behind the farmhouse and turn right onto the track which will lead you along to Holin-Bush Farm.

Follow the track alongside this second farmhouse until, at a modern barn, you reach a point where there is a distinct corner. Instead of following the track round to the right, cross the stone stile in front of you. Walk across the pasture field, making your way down the field, along the central depression which runs the length of the field and descend the bank-side to a gated footbridge.

On the other side, turn right and walk up into a pasture. Head across to the telegraph pole. From here, keep going in the same direction to a gateway. Pass through and cross the small pasture beyond to a further gate beside a public footpath sign.

Turn left onto the farm track and then almost immediately right where a public bridleway is indicated to Great Fry-up Dale. Follow this around a large barn.

Walk alongside the barn with the slope down to the stream on your right. Keep going along the bridleway until it brings you up to a farm track via a gate. Turn right along this track and come to the line of the dismantled railway.

Across the disused railway are a minor stream and, further to your right, a deep gulley. The path you want passes up between these two as a discernible green route. Keep the minor stream always on your left as you follow the trodden path up to a large boulder at the top of the gulley which has so far always been on your right. Bearing right, across the stream which feeds the deep gulley, follow the line of low cairns you can see until, by the fourth, you cross to a stone boundary marker. From this, you should be able to see the path ahead of you as a green strip through the heather.

Follow this strip, bearing rightward, until, at the top of the gentle rise, you can see occasional traffic passing along the minor road you are approaching. You can now identify a marker post and stone by the road. Make your way to these.

Cross the minor road and continue straight on, as indicated by a public bridleway sign. Begin walking through the gulley here and you will soon find the path quite evident across the moor top through the heather. You will come on to the stone George Gap Causeway and follow this, beyond a break in the stones as you cross a water course, until you come across a track leading from right to left across your way.

This path follows the line of boundary markers between the parishes of Danby and Rosedale which take the form of stones capped with white. Turn left along the black, peaty path and follow it until it comes to a minor road. Turn right and walk alongside the road. Carry on round the left-hand bend where there is a junction with a single track road, and on to the White Cross on your left.

Turning left opposite the White Cross, make your way along the public bridleway to the road which runs along Blakey Ridge and turn left along it to the Lion Inn.

Walk 6: Robin Hood's Bay

Route: Robin Hood's Bay – Cleveland Way – Rain Dale – Pursglove Stye – Hawsker Bottoms – Railway Path – Robin Hood's Bay

Distance: 6^1/$_2$ miles

Map: O.S. Outdoor Leisure 27, North York Moors Eastern Area (NE Sheet)

Start: The Laurel (Grid reference 953048)

Access: There is no vehicle access to the old part of the village at the cliff base, but two public car parks are provided at the top, so if you cannot find space in the one at the turning roundabout, go back up the hill a little to the much larger car park there.

By bus, you can reach Robin Hood's Bay seven days a week using Tees route 93 from Middlesbrough, Whitby or Scarborough.

The Laurel (0947 880400)

Built around 1750, the Laurel is one of the smallest pubs in North Yorkshire and has a friendly atmosphere enhanced by the availability of pub games – shove halfpenny and bar skittles, also darts. There is a quiz night on Wednesdays. Prominently set at a corner of the main street (New Road), you should find the Laurel easily.

There is a small family room and the main bar, which was carved from the living rock. Brasses and old pictures around the walls add to the general atmosphere of cosy conviviality.

Opening hours are 12 noon to 11pm Mondays to Saturdays. On Sundays there is a break in sessions from 3pm to 7 pm, and the usual earlier closing at 10.30 pm. Four cask conditioned ales are on offer – Old Peculier, Ruddles Best Bitter, Directors and John Smiths, and there are sandwiches at lunchtime.

The Dolphin Hotel (0947 880337)

Along the street from the Laurel, but with its main entrance around the corner on King Street, the Dolphin prides itself on being a no frills, old fashioned ale house. There is a varied selection – John Smiths Magnet and Bitter, Courage Directors, Websters Bitter and Mild and Ruddles are the basic menu, though they are not all available at once, with guest beers making special appearances too.

Bar meals, including local sea-food, may be had at weekends and in the evenings, also at lunchtime in the holiday season. A dining room is available on request. The Dolphin opens it doors from 11am to 11pm at holiday times and every Friday and Saturday. At other times, hours are 12 noon to 3pm and 7 to 11 pm.

Robin Hood's Bay

The pan-tiled roofs of the stone cottages of Bay Town, as it is locally known, huddle prettily against the cliffs around a scramble of narrow little stone alleyways. The road down is not as steep a descent as at Staithes (see Walk 15), though it is a rather more gentrified, even slightly touristy place now, whatever its smuggling, fishing past may have been.

What about the name? It dates from Tudor times at least, but there is no real link that can be established with the legendary outlaw.

Author Leo Walmsley was resident in Bay Town at the turn of the century and used it, or its fictionalised equivalent Brambleweick, as the backdrop to his novels Three Fevers, Phantom Lobster and Sally Lunn.

The Walk

From the Laurel, head up the road, out of the village and past the first public car park on the left, at the top of the hill. Continue along the road beyond the junction with the Fylingdales road until you reach the right-hand bend opposite the second public car park.

Take the street leading to the right, following the Cleveland Way marker-post. At the end of the street the Cleveland Way carries straight on to a kissing gate and a grass path between a hedge and a wire fence.

Coming to a second kissing gate, pass through into a pasture field. Walk along the right-hand edge of this field alongside a wooden fence and a hedgerow beyond which the cliff drops away to the sea. On your right you will come to a National Trust information board about this Rocket Post Field. From here rockets were fired until 1980 to be used as targets for practice by the Coastguard rehearsing rescue procedures.

At the boundary of Rocket Post Field you cross a stile and continue along the cliff top, separated from the edge by a wood fence and hedgerow. Coming to a further stile, you dip down a little, and then climb back to come to another three stiles to be crossed as you carry on along the Cleveland Way.

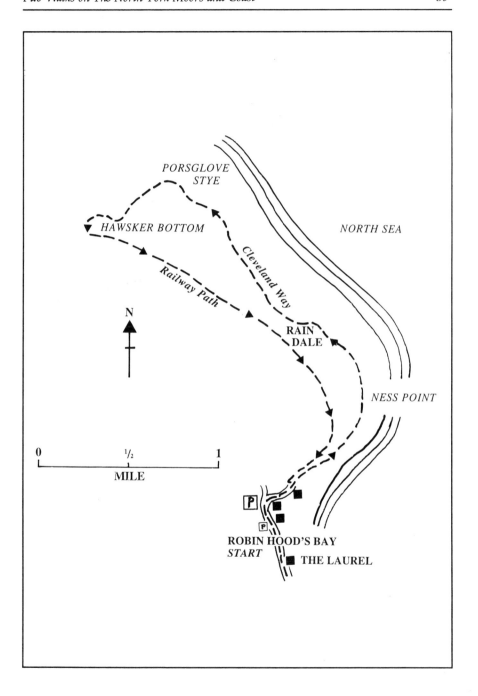

PORSGLOVE
STYE

HAWSKER BOTTOM

Cleveland Way

NORTH SEA

Railway Path

N

RAIN
DALE

NESS POINT

0   ¹/₂   1

MILE

P

ROBIN HOOD'S BAY
START

THE LAUREL

By now, you will find that the cliff top is now open to your right – there is no longer a fence between you and it. Keep following the cliff-top path, with the dry stone wall to your left, enjoying dramatic views of the scenery of this stretch of the Cleveland Heritage Coast.

The path leads you over a narrow, hand-railed, wooden footbridge across a gulley containing a stream. Following the path up the next rise, you will come to a divide in the ways. Ignore the waymarked path leading off to your left, and continue along the cliffs.

The track ascends a staircase of steps cut into the earth and then takes you through the National Trust property of Ness Point. Leaving this by the first of a series of stiles, simply continue to follow the cliff-top path with its breath-taking views.

Continually following the dry stone wall and wire fence to your right, you come to a stile leading you into an open section with no barrier between you and the cliff edge. Cross the second stile you reach at the end of this strip of rough ground, and find that the cliff path is again separated from the edge by a wire fence. Follow this fence-line for the moment.

Leave the Cleveland Way at a three-way marker point, and head inland towards Hawsker. You will now come to a waymark arrow directing you straight ahead towards a caravan park. Coming to the bottom end of this sloping caravan site, walk up the left-hand side of the central grass island.

Having walked all the way up between the caravans, turn right at a waymark sign and pass the front of the main building of the Northcliffe Caravan Park. Now walk downhill along the lane to cross the bridge over Oakham Beck at Hawsker Bottom.

The lane will bring you round a definite left bend, with horse paddocks on your left. Having rounded this bend, turn left onto the Railway Path, following, as the name suggests, the line of the dismantled railway. This used to run along this coast, south from Whitby and crossed the lane you have been walking along at right angles by the caravan site.

Pass through a wooden gate and then simply follow the track all the way along to Robin's Hood Bay. The Railway Path is never more than a field or two away from the cliff edge, so there are fine sea views along this stretch of the walk too.

As you enter the village, you will find that the path is diverted left, away from the line of the old railway. This is waymarked. You now find yourself back at the street where you started along the Cleveland Way earlier.

At the end of the street, turn left and descend back into the old village.

Walk 7: Castleton

Route: Castleton – Dibble Bridge – Foul Green Farm – Commondale – Moorside – Box Hall – Castleton.

Distance: 6 miles

Map: O.S. Outdoor Leisure 26, North York Moors Western Area (NW Sheet)

Start: The Downe Arms, Castleton (Grid reference 687081)

Access: There are British Rail stations at Commondale and Castleton on the Middlesbrough to Whitby line. In summer there are four trains a day, including Sundays. Normally, you will need to request on-train staff to stop. There is also a winter service. For information, ring BR on Darlington (0325) 355111.

The Moorsbus service from Middlesbrough, Helmsley, Pickering, and Whitby calls at Castleton which lies near the head of Eskdale, four miles south of the A171 Guisborough to Whitby road, on summer Sundays and Bank Holidays. For further details ring Tees and District on 0642 210131

The Downe Arms (0287 660223)

The Downe Arms is a stone built pub of 18th century vintage in the High Street. It retains a traditional atmosphere with stone walls, beams and large open fires and offers Youngers Scotch Bitter and No 3, also Witches Brew, occasionally. Bar meals are available until 9.30pm, and there is a two-course Sunday lunch.

Opening hours are from 7pm to 11pm Monday to Friday, 12 noon to 3pm and 7pm to 11pm Saturdays, and 12 noon to 3pm and 7pm to 10.30pm Sundays.

The Downe Arms

Castleton

Today a comparatively peaceful, if quite large, Moors village, Castleton was formerly busier with a weekly market and local weaving industry, now closed. There are still a variety of local services along its High Street, however, so that functionally at least it continues to approach the status of a town. The railway station remains and the annual show is held by the River Esk in mid-September.

Commondale

Commondale is striking for its unusual (for this area) number of brick buildings, reflecting its past as an important brickmaking centre. The pub here is the Cleveland Inn which is an interestingly old-fashioned free house with beer garden, but which does not, unfortunately, serve real ale.

The Walk

Coming out of the Downe Arms, turn left along the main street of Castelton. Keep going until you reach the Moorland Hotel at High Castleton. Opposite are two footpaths descending the grassy slope towards the River Esk. Take the leftward of these two paths and walk down to the minor road. Turn left and carry on along New Road to the crossroads.

Turn left and down to cross Dibble Bridge. Continue up the slope, passing Dibble Bridge Farm on your left and Maddy House on your right, before turning right towards Commondale. Walk alongside this surfaced, very quiet minor road on the grassy verge which separates it from the heather. Crossing the open moor this roadside section has good views over the dale. The road dips down into Commondale and over the bridge across Commondale Beck. Pass a house on the right called the Diving Duck and then walk under the small stone railway bridge.

Crossing a second stream, the road curves left up to Foul Green Farm. Bearing left down the road would bring you into Commondale village. Otherwise, turn right alongside the farm and towards the station – this is signposted on the side of the farm. Just past the farm, carry straight on past a five-barred gate which leads onto a path down to the station. Follow the bridlepath straight ahead before curving steeply left. Keep following the bridleway left, ignoring a five-barred gate leading to a stile, and pass along the ash track between a pair of dry stone walls.

Carry on along the bridleway, enjoying glorious views down over Eskdale, to and through a five-barred gate across the way. Coming into a fern-floored deciduous woodland, pass through a gate in a dry stone wall and follow the ash track as it bends slightly down to the right and past the stone-built farmhouse of Moorside.

Follow the bridleway as it curves left to a dry stone wall and on past the red-tiled Boxhall, set next to Winnow Hall. Arriving at the surfaced minor road next to the white gates of Firbank, follow the road downhill into Castleton, under the railway to the junction. Turn left here and follow the road back up into Castleton village – the Downe Arms is to your right when you reach the T-junction in the village centre.

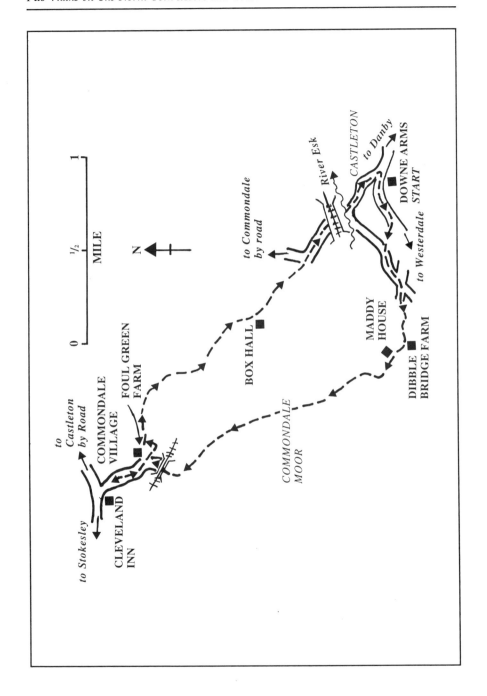

Walk 8: Danby

Route: Danby – Moors Centre – Duck Bridge – Danby Castle – Crossley
Gate – Forester's Lodge – Stonebeck Gate – Ainthorpe Rigg – Ainthorpe
– Danby

Distance: $5^3/_4$ miles

Map: O.S. Outdoor Leisure 27, North York Moors Eastern Area (NE
Sheet)

Start: The Duke of Wellington (Grid reference 707086)

Access: Danby station lies along the British Rail Esk Valley line, so the
village can be reached by train from Middlesbrough and Whitby.
Moorsbus services from Middlesbrough, Darlington, Helmsley, Whitby
and Pickering call at Danby Lodge Moors Centre on Sundays and Bank
Holidays in summer. Tees and District bus company (0642 210131) and
East Yorkshire Motor Services (0482 27146) can give up to date details.

The Duke of Wellington (0287 660351)

A family-run country inn, the Duke of Wellington dates from the 18th
century and supposedly changed its name after the Duke used the inn as
a staging post and for recruiting soldiers. The unusual shape of the
present inn is because it has absorbed neighbouring buildings, including
the village meeting room, a shop and a farmhouse and stable.

The bar has a real fire and Camerons Strongarm, Banks Bitter and John
Smiths Magnet are served. A range of home cooked food is available
with vegetarian choices and there is a separate restaurant – the Waterloo.

Danby

A lovely village set in the heart of Eskdale, Danby's two principal
monuments lie outside the village along the route of this walk. Duck

Bridge is a Medieval pack horse bridge thought to date from the 14th century and restored by George Duck some 400 years later.

The Duke of Wellington

Danby Castle is also 14th century in origin, though now ruined and part of a working farm, so not open to the public, though clearly visible from Castle Lane. Once the home of Catherine Parr, sixth wife of Henry VIII, it is claimed that the king travelled to Danby to woo her.

Today, one of the rooms is still used as the meeting room of the Danby Court Leet, who are the body responsible for managing the common land of Danby on behalf of the Lord of the Manor.

The Moors Centre

The Moors Centre is at Danby Lodge, a former shooting lodge of the Lord of the Manor of Danby, less than a mile east of Danby, and on the route of this walk. Set in substantial grounds, it must have been quite a palatial shooting lodge. Inside there is a permanent audio-visual exhibition about the Moors, a book and souvenir shop, cafe, brass rubbing room and a changing exhibition. Outside in the grounds is an adventure playground and map and compass pathfinder course. There is also a garden to stroll around, stocked with plants which grow wild in the National Park, including the three types of heather to be found – ling, bell heather and cross leaved heather.

The Moors Centre (0287 660644) is open every day from April to October from 10am to 5pm, and from November to March at weekends only 11am to 4pm. Admission is free.

The Walk

Begin from the signpost at the road junction next to the Duke of Wellington. Walk along the road in the direction of the Moors Centre. This is Lodge Lane and it will take you up and then down and round a right-hand bend to the Moors Centre itself on your left.

Opposite the Moors Centre car park, a signposted footpath leads straight over a field with a wire fence on your right. Follow this and cross the footbridge you reach on the other side. Continue along the field boundary and then over the level crossing to walk up to a stile and so to the road.

Turn left and follow this minor road as it bends right and passes the junction by the packhorse Duck Bridge. Keep going along the lane until you pass first the ruins of Danby Castle and its modern-day farm and then Crossley Gate Farm on your left.

Just past this second farm, turn left onto the signposted public footpath and down the side of Little Fryup Dale and through a gate to the beck at the bottom. Cross this and continue along the path and through two gates, following it round to the right until you come to imposing, and apparently abandoned, Forester's Lodge – a stone-built, solitary building. Pass through the gate, and head left up the green lane to turn right, still along a green lane. Follow this lane along to Stonebeck Gate Farm where you emerge onto a minor road. Turn right and walk up to the road junction, ignoring the signposted public bridleway on your left by

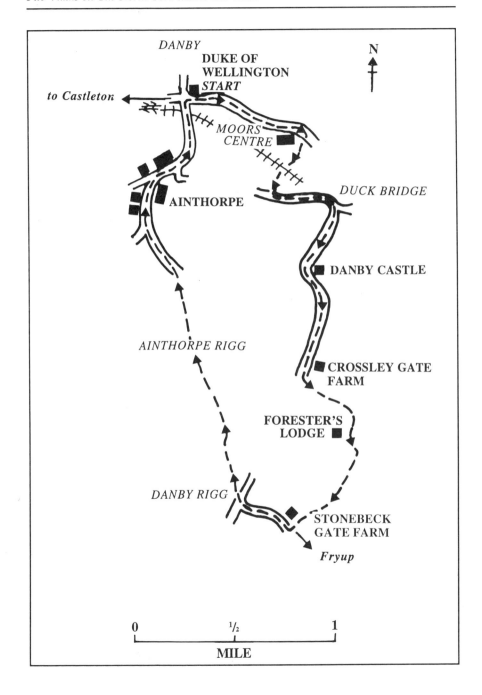

the cattle grid.

At the junction itself is the bridleway you want. Signposted, it takes you up the side of Ainthorpe Rigg at an oblique angle. Once on the flatter land at the top of the ridge, you will find that the track follows a series of cairns and standing stones which help guide you straight ahead all the way to a minor road.

Arriving at this road at a bend, turn left and walk down, past the tennis court, through the hamlet of Ainthorpe. Bear right all the way to the end of Brook Lane where you join the road leading to Danby.

After this, follow the road round to the left and across the River Esk, passing the railway station at Danby as you climb gradually through the village, back to the Duke of Wellington.

Walk 9: Glaisdale

Route: The Angler's Rest – Hart Hall – Bank House Farm – Postgate Farm – Postgate Hill – Broad Leas – Meadowfield – Glaisdale – The Angler's Rest.

Distance: $5^3/_4$ miles

Map: O.S. Outdoor Leisure 27, North York Moors Eastern Area (NE Sheet)

Start: The Angler's Rest (Grid reference 781054)

Access: The Angler's Rest is a road-side hostelry halfway down the half-mile bank from Glaisdale village to Glaisdale railway station. The latter is on the Esk Valley line and allows access by train from Whitby and Middlesbrough.

By car, you will find Glaisdale 3 miles south of the A171 Guisborough to Whitby road, turning off at Wilks Rigg (GR 797085).

The Angler's Rest (0947 87261)

A good climb up from the Esk to it, anglers are likely to need a rest by the time they reach this 17th century stone-built, real fire inn. Previously known as the Three Blast Furnaces – there were ironworks in Glaisdale village in the last century, the premises began life as farmhouse for the 7 acres of land surrounding the pub. This enables the Angler's Rest to offer camping, as well as accommodation, to its fishing, cycling, walking clientele.

Real ales on offer are Theakstons Best and Old Peculier, Tetley Bitter and Strongarm from Camerons. As well as Sunday lunch, the Angler's has sandwiches and bar meals available from Sunday evening to Friday lunchtime and a reasonably-priced à la carte menu on Friday and Saturday evenings.

Opening is 11am to 2.30pm and 7pm to 11pm weekdays, and 12 noon to 3pm and 7pm to 10.30pm on Sundays.

Glaisdale

The quiet and picturesque dale of Glaisdale runs south west north east from Glaisdale Head to the village of Glaisdale. This settlement is strung out along $1^1/_2$ miles of minor road from High Leas down to Carr End and Glaisdale Station, sited at the confluence of the tributary Glaisdale Beck with the Esk, by Beggar's Bridge (Walk 10).

The Hart Hall Hob

Early on this walk, you will pass by Hart Hall, site of one of the Moors best-known 'hob' legends,

The hobs of this region were a kind of Yorkshire leprechaun. For the most part they were helpful, bearded goblins who would help farm-folk with their daily tasks, but doing so shyly and unobserved, by night. They were believed to have a deep aversion to clothing, which they considered an encumbrance, and, therefore, to go about their tasks naked.

The farmer of Hart Hall, so the story goes, found himself in a fix when his hay wagon became stuck, and despite all the efforts of his workers, could not shift it. As darkness fell, there was nothing for it but to leave the hay on the cart overnight and hope it did not rain. The following morning, the farmer awoke to find all the hay neatly stacked by the hob.

One of the farm workers then became obsessed with catching a glimpse of the secretive hob, and one night managed to do so when he heard the hob threshing corn. Surprised to see the hob without anything to wear, he persuaded his fellow hands to make a suit of clothes for their nocturnal assistant. However, the hob did not appreciate their gift, and, realising he had been spied upon, took offence and left Hart Hall for ever.

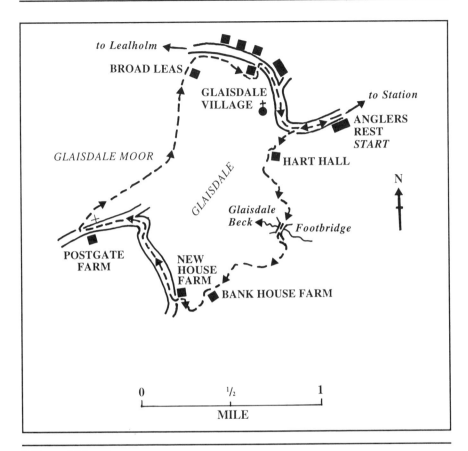

The Walk

Standing with your back to the Angler's Rest, turn left and head along the road almost as far as the tennis court. Just before you reach the tennis court, the public footpath you want is signed off to the left. Follow the path over a stile and into a pasture field. Here you will see a copse of tall trees diagonally across the field on a knoll. Make towards these, following the field edge.

From the copse, follow the hedgerow to your left almost to the corner at Hart Hall, until, across in the right-hand corner of the field, you can see a footpath waymark sign on a gate post. Walk around the pasture edge to this sign.

Pass through the gateway and turn left to walk along the edge of the pasture with trees and a dry stone wall to your left. Reaching a wooden farm gate, pass through it and carry straight on over the track to climb over a waymarked ladder stile opposite. Then bear left to walk along the field edge, with the hedgerow on your left. Come to a further stile and cross it. Keep straight on, through a first gateway, a few yards beyond which is a second.

Turn left at this second gateway, but avoid going through it. Instead turn left just in front of it and walk down the field with the hedgerow on your right. Directly behind you now is a green lane which leads to Red House.

You will find a line of stones marking your way to the field bottom where there is a gate, waymarked to direct you to the right. You immediately come upon a second gate, and go through it to walk straight along the grassy path with a hedgerow to your right. You will now find yourself looking up the length of Glaisdale.

The track then takes you leftwards and between two rows of hedges. At the end of this lane, you will arrive at a bridleway waymarker guiding you to the right and through a single wooden gate.

In front of you a line of laid single stones shows the way down the slope between two wire-fenced fields. You will emerge at a further single gate with adjacent stile. Negotiate these and head towards Glaisdale Beck and the footbridge which crosses it.

On the other side of the footbridge, head up and to the left, keeping the hedgerow on your left, walking around the edge of a pasture. Reach the corner and follow the hedge around to the right until you reach a waymark arrow on a massive old oak. Bear left at the oak tree and walk around the edge of the next pasture field, initially to the right and then uphill, keeping the hedgerow on your right all the way.

Reaching a three-way guidepost, by going through the gate you reach on your right, choose the bridlepath which takes you along the lower route up Glaisdale. Having come through the gate then, turn left and walk along the green bridleway along the top edge of the pasture you have now entered. This brings you through a waymarked metal gate, across the middle of the succeeding pasture, through a second gate, round to the right and then left beyond a third gateway. Reaching another gate, follow the track straight on along the pasture edge, with the wire fence on your left.

Beyond a still further gate, the track bends to the left as it continues to follow the hedgerow all the way on to the slope at the foot of Bank House Farm. Here you will come across a stile on your left. Ignore this and continue along the track through a gate. Follow it as it curves left, back on itself, as it ascends the slope by means of a hair-pin bend.

Reaching Bank House Farm, take the right-hand track leading you downhill, also further up the dale. The track bends right and down towards New House Farm. Just before reaching the farm buildings themselves, the track bends left and brings you onto a surfaced lane.

Turn right along this lane and follow it across the dale to the cattle grid where it joins the minor road. Head left along this road and walk along past Postgate Farm, ignoring a minor lane leading obliquely right and up, and passing Alexandra Cottage, also on your right.

Having passed Postgate Farm, Wesleyan Cottage on your left and the chapel on your right, join the public bridleway which is signposted off to the right. This grass track will take you up-slope, at an angle, behind the chapel graveyard.

Through a waymarked gate, follow the grassy bridleway as it continues to rise alongside a dry stone wall on your right to the open moor. Then, as the dry stone wall falls away to your right, continue up the hill and across a track which crosses your route.

Keep going to the small old quarry spoil-heaps at the top. Follow the grass track around the back of these and a few yards behind the top edge of the old quarry workings.

Coming to a dry-stone-walled enclosure on your left, keep following the grassy bridleway across the moor top until you reach a green public bridleway sign. Bear left , away from the line you have been following and join the ash track which takes you to a second waymark post. At this, bear left again, off the ash track and onto a green way from which you can see across to the Esk Valley. The path will bring you down to the corner of a wire fence which you should round to come to a metal gate. Through the gate, walk along the track and pass the stone-built cottage of Broad Leas on your right. Arriving at the minor road, you will see a ladder stile on your right.

Crossing the ladder stile, the waymarked path takes you along the back of the cottages of the upper part of Glaisdale village. Emerging, four fields later, alongside a large building used as a coal depot, you should turn left and come down to the Greens.

Turn right here onto the main minor road through the village and follow it down, along the main street, beyond the upper part of the village and tennis court, back to the Angler's Rest.

Walk 10: Egton Bridge

Route: Egton Bridge – Broom House Farm – Limber Hill Farm – Beggar's Bridge – East Arncliff Wood – Delves Farm – Hall Grange Farm – Key Green – Egton Bridge

Distance: 4^1/$_2$ miles

Map: O.S. Outdoor Leisure 27, North York Moors Eastern Area (NE Sheet)

Start: Postgate Inn (Grid reference 805054)

Access: Egton Bridge lies in the Esk Valley 3 miles south of the A171 Guisborough to Whitby road. The Esk Valley railway, which runs from Middlesbrough to Whitby, and is operated by British Rail, is an ideal means of access to the Postgate Inn which is right by the little station. Alternatively, Egton Bridge can be reached from Whitby by the C6 Tees Clipper minibus service, Mondays to Saturdays.

Postgate Inn (0947 85241)

This traditional country pub, named after Father Nicholas Postgate, last of the Catholic English Martyrs and on the site of whose home the inn stands, offers a cosy, authentic atmosphere warmed by a real fire. Bed and breakfast accommodation is available, and fishing can be arranged along the River Esk. Children and dogs are welcome. The building itself is ivy-clad and stone-built and there are tables in the garden.

Real ales offered are Camerons Strongarm and Traditional, alongside Tetley Bitter and featured guest beers including Burton Ale and Flowers. Opening hours from March to October are from 11am until 11pm, but these shorten in the winter months to 11am to 3pm and 6pm to 11 pm.

Most food is home-made and bar meals and sandwiches are available lunchtimes and evenings. Restaurant meals are also served in the evening and there is a traditional Sunday lunch, though bookings are advisable.

The Horseshoe Hotel

Horseshoe Hotel (0947 85245)

Set in $1^1/_2$ acres of grounds on the south side of Egton Bridge, the Horseshoe Hotel serves Theakstons Old Peculier, XB and Best Bitter, as well as Tetley Bitter and a weekly change of guest beer. It is open from 11am to 3.30pm and 6.30am to 11pm, with bar meals served 12 noon to 2pm and 6.30pm to 9pm, which are home-made and cooked to order from local supplies. Log fires provide a welcome warm in winter months and the splendid grounds are a beautiful setting for the outdoor drinker in more balmy times.

Egton Bridge

Quiet and picturesque on the River Esk, the village of Egton Bridge, whose annual Gooseberry Show is held on the first or second Tuesday in

August, is an ideal little railway halt. The Victorian Catholic church of St Hedda is interesting for its painted stations of the cross along the south exterior wall and for the Postgate Shrine.

Beggar's Bridge

This medieval stone packhorse bridge was rebuilt around 1620. It forms an integral part of this walk as it arches over the River Esk at Glaisdale. The legend of Beggar's Bridge concerns the identity of the beggar.

A poor country lad from Glaisdale, Tom Ferris, fell in love with a girl who lived on the other side of the Esk, but he was deemed unsuitable by the girl's father – a wealthy farmer. So, he left Eskdale to seek his fortune, found it and returned to build the bridge over to his sweetheart and marry her. Rather like that other fortune hunter Dick Whittington, Tom became mayor of a great city, but of Hull in his case, not London.

The Walk

From the Postgate Inn, walk along the road under the stone railway bridge and turn right along the minor road which is signposted to Glaisdale. Continue along this road beyond the village, River Esk to your left.

Following the road as it bends right under a stone railway bridge, walk up the hill and past Broom House Farm on your left. Just past the farm is a white gate on your left. Ignore this, but follow the footpath sign beside you which directs you up the road. As the road bends left, you will see a stile on your left which you should cross into a field. There is a sign here, but it is quite low and you will need to be on the lookout for it.

Now at the apex of a triangular field, follow the edge alongside the largely coniferous woodland, wire fence on your left. Reaching a corner in the wire fence, you will see a waymark post straight ahead of you. Make for this post. The path then leads down and up the sides of a gulley, to a waymark arrow directing you upward to the left. This takes you diagonally across a pasture clearing.

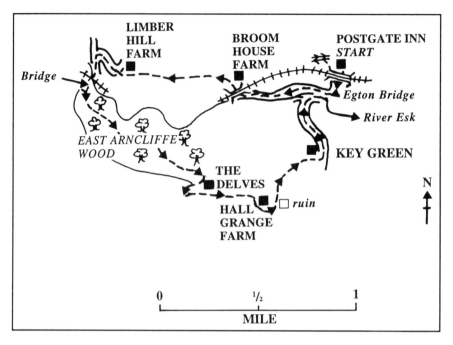

Ahead of you is the path to follow leading into the woods across a stile beside a waymarker arrow. Walk straight through the woods along the clearly trodden path until you reach the stile at the other side. Cross this into a pasture and keeping the wire fenced field boundary on your left, come to a further wooden stile in the top corner of the field.

Crossing the stile onto a track, carry straight on to begin with, towards the buildings of Limber Hill Farm. Just before you reach the farmyard, you will find a small triangle of open pasture land on your left. Walk across this, following the hedgerow on your left, past a telegraph pole, to a wooden gate at the apex of the triangle.

Pass through the gate and turn right to a second gate which leads you onto the road at a very sharp corner. Turn left and head downhill along the minor road.

Keep following the road downhill, not turning right, until you find it running parallel to the Esk, this time on your right. As the road bends right across the Esk, you carry straight on along the track on the left bank of the river to distinctive Beggar's Bridge.

Cross this medieval stone bridge to the railway bridge on the other side. Pass through the arch to the left of the arch taken by the road to a footpath waymarker post.

Follow the guidance given by this sign and cross the footbridge next to the ford. Pausing for a moment on this footbridge, it is worth contemplating the number of different river crossings within yards of each other at this quiet rural spot. Climb the wooden-edged cut steps and follow the waymarking leftward along the Esk Valley Walk, which here is part of the Coast to Coast long distance route.

An apparent division of the ways here is merely illusory – the two branches join again over the brow of the rise. Follow the path through East Arncliff Wood until the way divides. One choice bears left, hard by the stream, and the other, which you follow, is the main path up through the woods, indicated by a waymark arrow on a tree.

There are few choices to make as you amble through this fascinating wood, where in early autumn in you can see a profusion of nuts, berries and toadstools. Where there is a fork, just before the edge of the wood, take the right hand upward option.

Reaching the road, turn right and walk uphill along the road, following the bend round to the right at the Delves. Around the subsequent left bend, with its panoramic view back down Eskdale, you will see, as the trees thin, a public footpath sign, the first of two at Delves Farm, pointing the way left.

Follow this first sign's guidance to a metal gate and then along a grass path between hedgerows to a waymark arrow which sends you down to the left. Descending a fern covered slope, you will find a further waymark arrow on the fence at the bottom.

Cross the stile here into woodland. The path continues down and straight ahead, initially over some stones, to a stile at the slope foot. Cross this stile and the green lane that you meet, to pass through the waymarked farm gate straight ahead.

The path then brings you down to a dry stone wall with stone stile to help you across. Carry on straight ahead, crossing over the farm track you come upon, keeping the hedgerow to your left.

At the bottom of the slope, a wooden stile leads you onto a footbridge and so into a further pasture on the other side of the stream. The path continues straight ahead with a wooden fence to your left.

Keep going in a straight line, allowing the trees along the stream bank to drift away from you on the left. Passing a telegraph pole to your left, the path dips down and then rises into a further pasture. Walk across this grassland to the dry stone wall opposite and cross a stile onto the track there.

Turn right onto the track and follow it to Hall Green Farm. The track passes through the farm, in front of the farmhouse, and then immediately bends sharp left through a wooden gate. Walk uphill along the edge of the pasture to a single stone building at the top. Turn left in front of this building and along the green lane to a wooden gate and then onto rougher land covered by ferns.

Bearing right, follow the footpath between a dry stone wall to the left and quite high hedgerows to the right. This brings you to a hurdle gate with a stile beside it, and then to a further stile to negotiate.

Following straight along the lane, you will come to Key Green where you should pass through the yard and come onto the minor road. Turn left down the hill and into Egton Bridge.

At the road junction, there is the driveway of the Horseshoe Hotel directly opposite you. Only about five yards down this drive, the waymarked footpath leads off to the right and down some steps, on the far side of a wooden rail.

Coming to a wooden hand-railed, stone path beside the Esk, pass underneath a white footbridge to the stepping stones. Cross these to an island and then over a second set to the far bank.

On the other side, follow the path straight ahead over a stone platform and up a few steps. You will find yourself behind a row of houses and should turn right and walk a few yards along to find a cut on your left which will take you to the road alongside the end house. At the road, turn right into the village centre, turning left at the junction to pass under the railway bridge to the Postgate.

The Postgate Inn

Walk 11: Lastingham

Route: Lastingham – Spaunton – Bottomfields Lane – Hutton-le-Hole – Mary Magdalene Well – Camomile Farm – Lastingham

Distance: $5^1/_2$ miles

Map: O.S. Outdoor Leisure 26, North York Moors Western Area (SW Sheet)

Start: Blacksmiths Arms (Grid reference 728906)

Access: Lastingham is $2^1/_2$ miles east of Hutton-le-Hole which is the best place to begin this walk if you are travelling by bus.

Hutton-le-Hole can be reached by the Moorsbus service on Sundays from the end of May to the end of September, and on Spring and Summer Bank Holiday Mondays. There is a once-weekly Wednesday service to both Hutton-le-Hole and Lastingham operated locally by H. Wilson; but this is really in the wrong direction – taking people into Kirkbymoorside for the market in the morning and returning to Lastingham and Hutton-le-Hole in the early afternoon.

For drivers, Lastingham is easily accessible from the A170 road between Kirkbymoorside and Pickering. Turn off about $1^1/_2$ miles east of Kirkbymoorside and follow the signs for the $3^1/_2$ mile drive north to the village.

Blacksmiths Arms (07515 247)

This is a real find, a genuine village pub, stone-built and with a traditional beamed interior, complete with original iron range in which the real fire is still lit, it is a focal point of local life.

Opposite the historic village church where St Cedd is buried, the Blacksmiths Arms is open from 11am to 11pm Mondays to Saturdays.

Sunday opening is 12 noon to 3pm and 7pm to 10.30pm. Bar meals range from soup and sandwiches to steak, and the blackboard choice can include game and rabbit pies and casseroles. The pub has its own bistro which opens Friday and Saturday evenings. There is seating outside and a pool/games room at the rear. A variety of hand-pulled beers are served including Bass, Stones, Websters Yorkshire and Theakstons bitters as well as guest beers, such as Hambleton, and Scrumpy Jack Cider which is also hand-pulled.

The Blacksmith's Arms

Lastingham

Quiet, stone-built Lastingham, has to be one of the prettiest villages in England, never mind North Yorkshire, and is well worth a visit. The abbey of Lastingham was founded by St. Cedd in A.D. 654 and on its site now stands the thirteenth century parish church whose impressive Norman interior is a reminder of its initial monastic intention.

The original monastery was destroyed by the Norse in the 9th century and it was not until the reign of William the Conqueror that an attempt to resurrect it was made, but not completed. Only the crypt was finished and it is this that survives.

Spaunton

Spaunton is a work-a-day but nonetheless pretty hamlet with stone houses scattered around the small green. Woodman's Cottage is dated 1695 and Spaunton Manor Cottages have an interesting dovecot, clearly visible from the walk.

Hutton-le-Hole

As its name implies, Hutton-le-Hole is nestled into a sheltered hollow of the moors. A truly green village, free roaming Black-face sheep keep its grass short on either side of Hutton Beck which wends its way the length of the village's street of stone cottages.

Ryedale Folk Museum (07515 367)

Revealing a thousand years of rural life in Ryedale, this open-air museum features actual buildings from Ryedale. These include thatched cottages, farm buildings, workshops with frequent demonstrations, an Elizabethan Manor House and the oldest photographic studio in Britain set out on a $2^1/_2$ acre site. The museum is open from the end of March to the beginning of November from 10.30am to last admission at 4.45pm.

The Walk

Emerging from the Blacksmiths Arms turn left, down the dip in the road and left again through the village, past Cedd's Well, to the crossroads by the telephone box. Turn right here and then right again where there is a No Through Road sign, walking with the stream to your left until you pass Harwood Cottage where the track curves left into a farmyard.

Instead of following the track into the farmyard, follow the waymarked grassy path up to the right, and through a wooden gate into woodland.

Keep following the main path upward, eventually to the left of a gulley and through a waymarked gate – the latter involving a slight turn right.

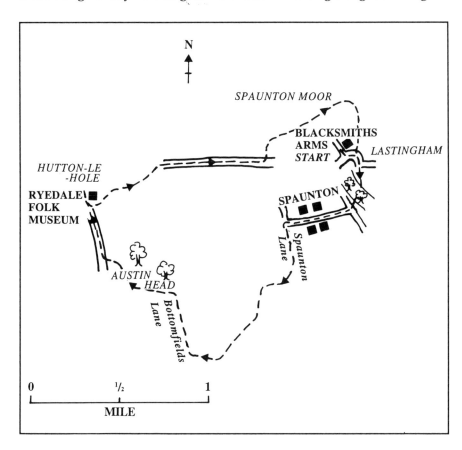

The gulley still to its right, the path brings you to a minor road junction. Take the road which is signposted to Spaunton, a quarter of a mile away. Having walked the length of linear Spaunton, turn left at the T-junction, past the No Through Road sign, onto the gravelly track of Spaunton Lane and through a gateway. Continue down the lane between the hedgerows and look carefully for a public footpath going off right. This is indicated by a low (about 3 feet high) sign next to an open gateway and opposite a patch of dry stone wall – the first break in the hedgerow on your left since you began to walk down Spaunton

Lane. At this point, turn right into the field and note the small disused quarry in the left-hand corner of the field which is marked on the OS map (725892). Follow the right-hand edge of the field, where the path is a reserved grass strip, right down to two right angled corners, first left and then right, to the field corner. Here there is a waymark sign taking you left along the dry stone wall to the right. The path has been diverted and may not match the line shown on your OS map.

Passing through a series of gaps in the hedges carry straight on along the edge of the next four fields, until you arrive at a stile five yards left of the corner of the last of these.

Cross the waymarked stile and walk along the right-hand edge of the next field and over the next waymarked stile into a patch of uncultivated shrubland. Then turn right onto the well-trodden bridleway, rather than going straight ahead over the next stile.

Follow the green lane, between hedgerows on either side, to a right angle. Continue to the right along the now-stoney Bottomfields Track to the next right angle where you turn left along the grassy way before it swings right and narrows. Walk along the path, down through the trees and through a gate until it swings round to the left and carries on downhill on to white racecourse style railings. You are now in Hutton-le-Hole and, turning right, can make your way along the main street.

Turn right just before the Ryedale Folk Museum onto the waymarked footpath next to Rose Crafts. This leads into a hotel car park and then branches right across the grass to the right of some wooden stable-like buildings and across a wooden stile into a field. Here you join a wider track and continue in the same direction toward a gate. The thatched buildings of the Ryedale Folk Museum are across the fence to your left.

At the gate, a waymarked wooden stile takes you into the next field – initially with the Folk Museum still on the left. The waymarked path continues straight ahead beyond the museum compound and across a further wooden stile and a field. Crossing this field there is a wire fence on your left.

Cross this small field to a gap between hedge and fence and, bearing left, keeping the hedge on your left, head toward a further gate with waymarked stile adjacent. The path crosses the next field and heads straight towards a wooden gate on the far side where you will discover a white gate leading onto a footbridge across Fairy Call Beck.

Walk over the bridge and onto a clearly trodden path up through the trees. Carry straight on to the wooden gate at the top of this path and, at the edge of the trees, through the gate to some unenclosed land. The path is evident at the top of the rise, curving round to the right past the telegraph pole. It leads you down past a waymark sign onto the minor road which we follow along in the same direction as we have been walking – eastward.

To the left of this road is open heather moorland which you have reached really comparatively effortlessly – an easy walk up from Hutton-le-Hole. Press straight on past High Cross House – a stone cottage on the right and continue along until the road bends right across a stone bridge toward a junction. At this bend, leave the road and follow the public footpath which is signposted on the left.

This brings you to a stile. Cross it and continue straight on at first, until the grass track bends around to the right. Following the track round, the boundaries of enclosed fields are to the right and open moorland is to the left. There are beehives along here.

On reaching Camomile Farm, the path is waymarked to the left towards a copse enclosed by dry stone walling. At the right-angled corner of this enclosure, follow the wall to your right, with open moor to your left. Follow the wall along and down into the valley of Hole Beck. Lastingham is now visible on the other side, across to your right.

Cross Hole Beck by means of the stepping stones and proceed along the path, keeping the dry stone wall on your right, until you reach a welcome wooden seat with views over to Lastingham's stone cottages. At the seat is a waymark post. Turn right and down into Lastingham along the downhill track and then road passing the Grange Hotel on your left and emerge onto the main street of Lastingham at the old Post Office. Turn right and pass Cedd's Well on your right. At the church turn right to the Blacksmiths Arms.

Near Hutton-le-Hole

Walk 12: Cropton

Route: Cropton – Mill Wood – Hunter Hill – Sinnington – Cliff Wood – Low Lane – Cropton

Distance: $5^1/_2$ miles

Map: O.S. Outdoor Leisure 27, North York Moors Eastern Area (SE Sheet)

Start: The New Inn (Grid reference 756888)

Access: Cropton village is $2^1/_2$ miles along Cropton Lane from the A171 Kirkbymoorside to Pickering road. Drivers should turn off at Wrelton, $4^1/_2$ miles east of Kirkbymoorside, and follow the signs to Cropton.

By bus, Cropton is accessible only by the locally operated Lockers Coaches (0751 73000) once weekly Monday service to and from Pickering market. Since this leaves Cropton mid- morning, to return at lunch-time, it is perhaps not much help unless you are camping or staying overnight.

The New Inn (07515 330)

An imposing, stone built pub just outside Cropton village, a little along the lane to Wrelton. If driving from there, you will reach it before the village.

The New Inn's claim to fame is that it has its own brewery, producing Cropton "2 Pints" Best Bitter (OG 1040). Of perhaps similar flavour, though much stronger, is Cropton Special Strong Bitter (OG 1060), and both use local well water. Also served in the pub is Scoresby Stout, named after a famous Whitby seafarer and whaler, as well as Tetley Bitter and Mild.

Open from 11am to 2.30pm and 6 to 11pm on Mondays to Saturdays in summer (12 noon to 2.30pm and 7pm to 10.30pm on Sundays), the New

Inn has winter sessions beginning an hour later Mondays to Saturdays. Winter Sunday opening is the same as in summer.

The pub has seen some recent extension, including a conservatory overlooking its beer garden. Food includes sandwiches and bar meals on

The New Inn

Monday to Saturday lunch-times and a carvery with bar meals for Sunday lunch. In the evenings bar meals are available from 6pm and the restaurant opens at 7 pm.

Cropton

The village itself lies a couple of hundred yards further along Cropton Lane, off to the right. There are two rows of cottages of local grey limestone flanking a noticeably wide single street. A quiet place, it seems well settled into the landscape, standing on the edge of Cropton Forest at the foot or "end" of Rosedale; in Moorspeak the blank end of a dale is the head, and the open end or mouth is the "end".

On the edge of the village are the remains of its motte and bailey castle which was sited to control the entrance to Rosedale.

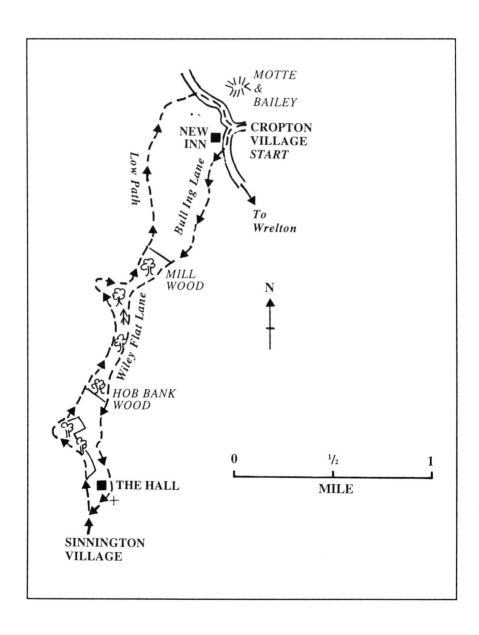

Sinnington

At the southern tip of this walk is the picturesque riverside village of
Sinnington. Linear in plan, it was sited at the bridging point of the River
Seven en route from Kirkbymoorside to Pickering, though mercifully
today's A171 by passes the village to the south, leaving it a sleepy
backwater. There is a very small packhorse bridge on the green which is
surrounded by pretty cottages spread around its fringe.

Sinnington Hall, which you pass as you approach the village, has as a
barn of some interest which may have been the Medieval Manor House.
The modern day church, surprisingly sited right by the Hall, is quite a
distance from the village proper.

The Walk

Coming out of the New Inn, you turn right and walk along the road a
little to the public bridleway sign. Turn right here into tree-lined Bull Ing
Lane.

Keep following the lane straight ahead, ignoring a footpath to the right if
you should see it – it is unmarked. You will arrive at a point where the
path divides into three ways, two of which lead through waymarked
gates. Take the middle way, involving you bearing rather then turning
right, through a gate into a field.

Follow this path diagonally over the pasture to a farm gate. Pass through
this and follow along the top edge of the next pasture to a single gate.
Then follow the path round to the left, at the top of a tree-covered slope,
until the path divides. Take the right-hand path curving right, along the
edge of the trees. After taking a leftward sweep, this brings you to a
single gate and into a more densely wooded area.

In this wooded area you will come to a parting of the ways and should
take the upper, left-hand fork. Continue straight on, past another
unmarked way on your right. On the next occasion, a path branches off
down to the right, ignore it again and carry straight on along the path
which is now on the edge of the woods.

At the end of the woods, you emerge in to a more open area with a field sloping down to your right. There is a waymarked stile leading across this field, but that is not the way you want. Instead, continue on the upper, left-hand path along the top of the slope with the hedgerow to your right.

There has been a wire-fenced field on your left. As you come to the end of this field, take a right and follow the lane downwards, between two hedges. Coming to a junction of paths where there is a waymarker, turn left along the lane to The Hall. Follow the track into the farmyard, round to the right and then the left, and onto the drive from the farm to Sinnington village. Pass the church on your left and come to the bottom of the lane. Turn left here and walk into Sinnington village to enjoy its picturesque riverside.

To continue the walk, go back to the bottom of the lane leading to the church. Carry straight on, past a 'no through road' sign and a row of brick-built cottages, to a choice of routes.

Take the bridleway to the left, down to the river. Walk along, through the trees, until the way divides again. Follow the footpath which takes you right, along the edge of the woodland.

Curving up, into and through the woods, coming to a crossing of paths, you continue straight on and follow the path down to a field. Cross the stile and walk along the grass track which crosses the middle of the pasture.

Where the track divides, take the right-hand fork and then curve left into the woods. A path will join from the left, but carry straight on, parallel to Cropton Beck, at the top of the bank-side, ignoring a further path to the right. The path then descends to river level and then bears right of a field between it and the beck. Walking along the bottom edge of the woods, you should ignore a path which branches steeply up to the right and come to a single wooden gate. Instead of going through the gate, bear right and follow the path up a gentle rise, keeping the wire fence on your left, until you reach a lane.

Turn right along the lane and walk up through the trees. You will come to a convergence of paths. One path joins from the right and there are two possible ways forward. Take the left fork and press on through the trees and down to a gate.

Beyond the gate, walk along the lane, hedgerow on either side, through a second gate to a wooden signpost. Follow the Cropton direction, straight on along a broader lane to a divide in the ways.

Keep going straight ahead, not right, here and along the base of the slope, as waymarked, along a lane between two hedgerows. Ignore a minor path leading right and cross a stile and then go through three gates in succession, to keep straight on until you come onto a farm track.

Again, carry straight ahead, through a further gate, until you emerge onto the minor road. Turn right alongside this and follow it uphill, back to the New Inn.

Walk 13: Levisham

Route: Levisham – Levisham Station – Newton Banks – Newton Dale – Farwath – Sleights Road – Levisham

Distance: 5^1/$_2$ miles

Map: O.S. Outdoor Leisure 27, North York Moors Eastern Area (SE Sheet)

Start: The Horseshoe Inn (Grid reference 833906)

Access: From the A169 Pickering to Whitby road, you can drive to Levisham via Lockton along a narrow and twisting minor road which is about 1^1/$_2$ miles long.

The North York Moors Railway is your public transport option. You can catch the privately-run steam trains from Pickering or connect with them from British Rail's Whitby to Middlesbrough service at Grosmont. NYMR trains operate from April to October. There is a talking timetable service on 0751 73535.

Alighting at Levisham Station, you could join this walk there, and call in at the Horseshoe Inn most of the way round. The station is 1^1/$_2$ miles from Levisham village and is at the foot of the steep side of Newton Dale.

The Horseshoe Inn (0751 60240)

Standing prominently at the top end of Levisham village green, flag pole and all, the Horseshoe Inn is unmissable. Arranged in front of the pub are picnic tables where you can sit with your drink and gaze down the length of the stone-built village.

Inside this 16th century family run inn, you will find Theakstons Ales (Old Peculier, XB, Best Bitter and Mild) on tap, as well as Tetley Bitter and occasional guest beers. Bar meals are home-made from local produce and are served seven lunchtimes a week from 12 to 2pm and the restaurant opens in the evenings (Tuesday to Saturday).

The pub has conventional opening hours of 11am to 3pm and 7 to 11pm and offers en-suite accommodation as well as camping at the rear.

The Horseshoe Inn

Levisham

Levisham village sits on its own raised plateau at the end of a tortuous lane leading up from the main road, via pretty Lockton. A green village, it consists of two ranks of solid stone cottages and farm on either side of quite a lengthy green sward. This near end-of-the-line, restricted site has helped keep commercialisation away from Levisham and it remains a quiet moorland village.

Newton Dale

The steep-sided and wooded gorge of Newton Dale is an overflow channel eroded by meltwater which spilled over from the lake which filled Eskdale to the north during glacial times. Ice from Scandinavia pressed against the end of Eskdale, so that the rising water sought out the lowest point to rush over and down to the more extensive Lake Pickering. This occupied what is today's Vale of Pickering, similarly dammed by ice from the frozen North Sea.

In the early nineteenth century, Newton Dale was viewed as the natural corridor along which to build the Whitby to Pickering railway. It is the Grosmont to Pickering stretch of this which is today preserved as the steam North York Moors Railway.

Although opened in the 1830s, it was not until the 1840s that steam locomotives were introduced, to replace horse drawn wagons, when George Stephenson's engineering feat was taken over by railway king George Hudson. The service survived until the Beeching cuts of the 1960s when it closed for 4 years, before enthusiastic restorers were able to start stock rolling again.

Levisham station lies $1^1/_2$ miles away from the high village in the floor of Newton Dale. It is passed by this walk which offers superb vantage points to see the steam trains in action as they ply up and down the dale.

The Walk

The Horseshoe Inn stands between the two roads of a fork at the northern end of the long green. Stand facing the front of the pub at this fork and begin by walking down the road to the left of both of the others. This takes you past a no through road sign.

Follow this road along, until it turns left. You, however, continue straight ahead along a public footpath over a stile. Cross this and walk along the track at the side of the field with a dry stone wall on your right.

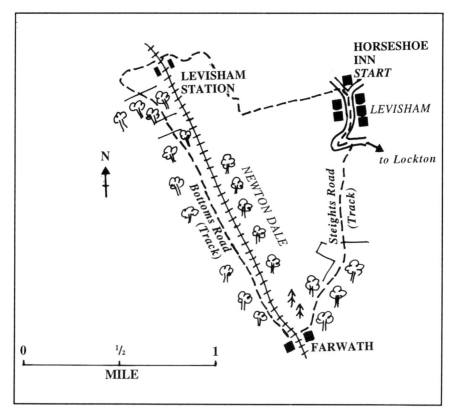

Come to a second stile, cross it and continue beside the dry stone wall to a third stile. Over this the way slopes away diagonally to your right. You can see that down ahead of you is the valley of Newton Dale. Follow the path around the slope until you pass a wooden seat with a fine view over Levisham Station. It then joins a definite incline which you follow down to a wooden signpost.

Turn left in the direction of the station. This involves going through a farm gate and walking along the edge of the field, at first across and then down the slope. As you are going down you will have a wire fence and hedgerow on your right.

At the bottom of the field pass through the single wooden gate by a sheep pen and enter the woods. Passing through a further gateway, you cross the beck in front of you to the road leading down to the station on your left.

Use the level crossing to cross the railway track beside the station's signal box. Continue straight along the lane on the other side of the tracks as far as the first bend where a waymarked gate leads you across a footbridge. Walk up one of the paths on the other side to the top of the first part of the slope. Here the way divides. Take the leftward leading path to go further up the slope until you emerge from the trees and onto a more gently sloping pasture.

Go along the wire fence edge of this as far as a track across your way which comes to a gate and stile. Cross the stile and follow the path downhill to a gate taking you into the woods and a division of the ways.

Take the right-hand fork and the clearly trodden path will bring you to another gate. Beyond, the path bears just slightly left downhill. Coming to a more open area at the bottom edge of the woods, the path curves round to the right a little and continues clearly ahead along the slope.

Pass through the next two gates and cross a pasture to a third gate – the second to be made of metal painted white. Cross a further pasture to a wooden gate and proceed along with a hedgerow to your right.

The railway line will be just down on your left beyond a reedy area as the path continues to lead you along and through a hedge into another pasture field. Crossing, this you can to see the river to your left. Then pass through a more-wooded area and just keep going along this Bottoms Road track until it is joined by another track coming down from the right. Turn left onto this track and follow it down towards the cottage you can see through the trees.

This is Farwath, where the footbridge takes you over the river to the railway line. Cross this to the other cottage on the other side of the level crossing. Continue along the lane past a bridleway which fords the stream to your left and come to a wooden gate. Turn left along the bank of the stream and follow the track as it curves up and left.

Enter the wood via a wooden gate and follow the track to a metal gate. On the other side you will be walking along a green lane to a pasture across which this Sleights Road track leads, in a little hollow of its own, between two rows of bushes.

At the other side of the pasture pass through a metal gate and continue along the track in front of you. Passing a stone boundary marker, the way proceeds between two lines of low trees and continues in similar fashion beyond a second stone.

Reaching a metal gate, there is a perhaps surprising view down to a solitary-towered church in the valley bottom. As you come through the gate, you will find, initially, a wire fence ending in a gateway. Rather than pass through the gateway itself, walk down the other side of the wire fence, keeping it on your left. There are trees and bushes on your right as you make your way down towards the church.

At the bottom of the path and opposite the church there is a wooden gate beside a weir. Go through the gate and walk along the stream bank to a footbridge. Cross this.

On the other side simply continue along the path directly ahead of you to pass the church and its graveyard on your left. The path then leads you between a high hedgerow, including holly bushes, on your right and a wire-fenced pasture to your left.

Climbing to a more significant track, turn right and follow it uphill to emerge onto a minor road by a public bridleway sign. Turn left and follow the road uphill into Levisham village. The Horseshoe Inn is at the far end of the green.

Walk 14: Saltergate

Route: Saltergate – Levisham Moor – Dundale Griff – Hole of Horcum – Saltergate

Distance: 5 miles

Map: O.S. Outdoor Leisure 27, North York Moors Eastern Area (SE Sheet)

Start: The Saltersgate Inn (Grid reference 852944)

Access: Saltergate is on the A169 Whitby to Pickering road, 9 miles south of Sleights, and about as far north of Pickering. You can reach it by bus using Yorkshire Coastliner (0653 692556) service 840/842 from York, Malton, Pickering or Whitby, seven days a week.

The privately run steam railway from Grosmont or Pickering provides another means of access for the Saltersgate Inn. Levisham station in Newton Dale is just over a mile away from Dundale Pond on this walk and train travellers could join it there. The North York Moors Railway Talking Timetable is on 0751 73535 and trains run from April to the end of October. Grosmont station is also on the British Rail Middlesbrough to Whitby line and so connections from these two are possible.

The Saltersgate Inn

The Legendary Saltersgate Inn, as proprietors Roger and Marie style it, is rich in murky history. The name Saltersgate comes from the days of salt smuggling, when the fishers of Staithes (Walk 15), Robin Hood's Bay (Walk 6) and Whitby, brought their fish to the inn to secretly salt it in the beer cellars. A bushel of salt was the equivalent of a month's income from fishing.

The story has it that an Inland Revenue official, watching the pub, single-handedly raided it to catch the fishermen in the act. They set upon him, murdered him and supposedly buried him under the fireplace. This is why, the legend says, the fire has never been allowed to go out in the iron range for 190 years, for fear that if it should, the spectre of the Revenue Man will rise again.

The Saltersgate Inn dates from 1648 and is open from 8.30am to 11pm in summer and, in winter, keeps similar hours, except for a three-hour closure from 3pm to 6pm. These hours reflect the wide range of food and refreshments on offer all day, including tea, coffee, scones, hot country broth, sandwiches and bar meals.

Real ales are Theakstons (Best Bitter, Old Peculier and XB), Bass and Camerons Traditional, and there are a beer garden and patio overlooking the moors.

Given its remote location, the Saltersgate Inn retains a gritty though warmly welcoming authenticity, and is a real walkers' pub with no pretensions to luxury. Nevertheless, it was a 1992 winner in the Yorkshire Pub of the Year competition, and extends its welcome to all-comers – children and dogs, hikers and bikers.

The Hole of Horcum

This natural amphitheatre, over 100m deep, is an impressive physical feature. It is variously thought to have been carved out of the land by the powerful rush of meltwater during the later Ice Age, or more sedately attributed to the sapping action of the springs which arise around its flanks, eroding over many thousands of years.

A combination of both is perhaps the true explanation although, according to local legend, it was scooped out by a giant as he grasped in anger for a sod to throw at his wife.

The Walk

From the Saltersgate Inn front door, turn right and walk alongside the main road, ignoring a public footpath on your right, as far as the sharp left-hand bend you can see ahead, at the top of the rise.

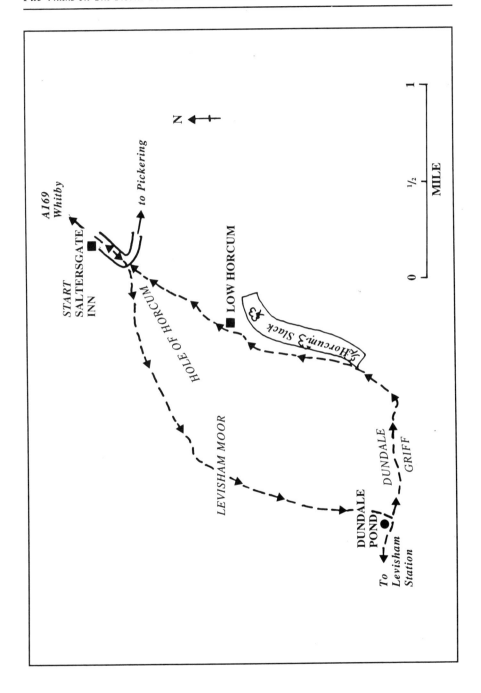

As you round this bend, you will see, virtually on the apex, a little gulley leading up to a wood rail fence. Walk up and, at the top, turn right over the stile onto the track which follows the top of the ridge.

Pass a little plaque, at foot-level on your right, announcing your entry into the Levisham Estate, and then just keep following the path until you come to Dundale Pond, some 2 miles or so further on. At the pond there is a marker post offering as many as 5 different directions. Take the one signposted to Dundale Griff. This involves you taking a left turn along the valley – this is the only downhill option on offer.

Walk the length of the valley of Dundale Griff. At the bottom you will find another waymarker sign. Turn left towards Saltergate, crossing a small footbridge. Reaching a second footbridge, cross it to find a waymark arrow directing you left along the stream bank.

Walk along with the stream on your left. The path parallels the stream, but gradually climbs away from it. Cross the stile you reach and follow the path round to a second waymarked stile which you can cross into a pasture field. Follow the path along the top edge of the field, initially, wire fence and woodland to your right. The path then begins to take a more central course across the pasture land, until it brings you to a waymark arrow on a post which simply directs you straight ahead.

Pass the boarded-up farmstead of Low Horcum on your right and come down to a waymarked wooden gate, beyond which your climb out of the Hole of Horcum begins.

Follow the path straight ahead of you, and up. The last part of the climb is along a rocky gulley, and this leads you to a ladder stile. Cross this and turn left.

Walk the few yards down to the hair-pin bend in the road, from which the Saltersgate Inn is again visible down in the dip.

Walk 15: Staithes

Route: Staithes – Port Mulgrave – Hinderwell Church – Dales Beck – Well Bank – Staithes

Distance: 5 miles

Map: O.S. Outdoor Leisure 27, North York Moors Eastern Area (NE Sheet)

Start: The Royal George, Staithes (Grid reference 783188)

Access: Staithes is half a mile north of the A174 Guisborough to Whitby road. Like many cliff-base fishing villages, Staithes village itself is kept as traffic free as possible, and so a car park is provided at the cliff top from which visitors can walk into the village below.

By public transport, Staithes can be reached by Tees buses from Middlesbrough, Guisborough and Whitby – service 256, seven days a week.

The Royal George (0947 841432)

On the High Street in Staithes, the Royal George serves real ales (Camerons Strongarm and Bitter, Burton Ale, Tetley Bitter) and bar meals in a traditional and friendly pub with low ceiling beams and cosy wood panelling. As you might expect, given that the licensee is himself a keen walker. Boots and rucksacks are welcome, as are dogs.

Inside the Grade II listed building are a bar, a snug used by local fishers and a lounge. Sunday lunches and evening bar meals are offered all year and bar meal lunches are available in summer.

Opening hours are 11am to 4pm and 7 to 11pm weekdays, 12 noon to 3 and 7pm to 10.30pm Sundays.

Staithes

A fishing village of narrow streets and alleys huddled at the bottom of the cliffs, Staithes clings to the steep valley sides of the Staithes Beck.

Captain James Cook worked here for 18 months from 1745 as assistant to a local merchant and is said to have developed his taste for the sea and ships while in Staithes.

Port Mulgrave

Port Mulgrave is a hamlet along the North Yorks and Cleveland Heritage coast. It grew when ironstone was mined here in the mid 19th Century to be shipped north to blast furnaces at Jarrow, on the Tyne. The two original terraces of cottages – Long Row and Short Row were built as homes for the ironstone miners.

The building of the harbour began in 1856. When Port Mulgrave's own ironstone reserves dwindled, it continued to serve nearby Grinkle Park Mine. Ironstone was taken along a narrow gauge railway, passing through 2 tunnels to reach Port Mulgrave, until 1917 when the mine was connected directly to the Middlesbrough – Whitby railway. In 1934 the harbour machinery was finally sold, though the breakwater was only destroyed in the Second World War – as an anti-invasion measure.

The 94 ha of land here is owned by the National Trust. It forms part of Enterprise Neptune – the Trust's campaign to save Britain's unspoiled coastline.

The Ship Inn (0947 840303)

Situated 600 yards inland from the cliff path down to the small remaining quay at Port Mulgrave, the stone-built Ship Inn is a family run free house. It serves morning coffee, sandwiches, toasties and bar snacks until 8.45pm , as well as real ale (Tetley, John Smiths Bitter, Youngers No. 3). There is a family room at the rear, as well as a separate dining room.

Inside, this local pub is quite open but traditional with an interesting collection of maritime pictures and an old pendulum clock ticking on the wall. The pictures include a reconstructional painting of Port Mulgrave as it was and old photographs of Whitby.

It makes a welcome port of call – especially if you have just climbed back up the cliff from the old harbour! You will find it open from 11am to 11pm Monday to Saturday and, on Sundays, from 12 to 3pm, when lunch is served, and from 7pm to 10.30pm. Bed and breakfast accommodation is available.

The Walk

From the Royal George, turn left along the cobbled High Street and follow the footpath around the front of the Cod and Lobster (another Real Ale pub serving Camerons and Tetley). Then, turn right up Church Street and past Captain Cook's cottage. Reaching the top of the street, which is a no-through road for traffic, take the footpath straight ahead to a flight of steps and then, at the top, a left along the way-marked Cleveland Way.

The path passes farm buildings on the right and leads you alongside a wire fence to a wooden stile. This is the first of a series of three, into grass fields, following the wire fence on your left until you reach the cliff top fence.

At the cliff top, turn right alongside the fence, keeping it on your left. Below are the beach and rocks of Brackenberry Wyke.

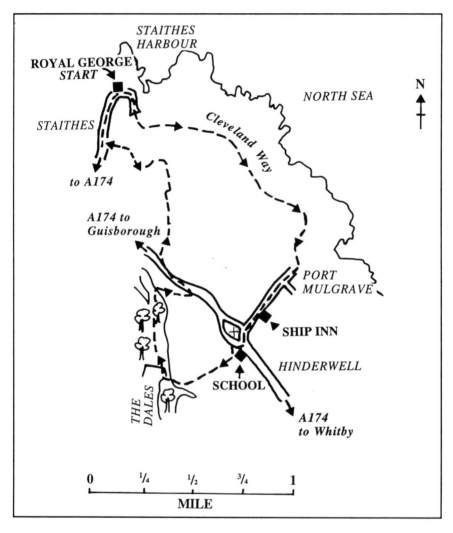

Crossing a wooden waymarked stile the cliff top path of the Cleveland Way offers splendid views down over the heather to the rocky shore. You can also see a five-bar gate next to the first stone-built houses of the hamlet of Port Mulgrave. Pass through the gap just to one side of this gate.

To the left a steep path drops down through National Trust land to the site of the harbour of Port Mulgrave and its short pier. Ignore this path, and follow the level main walk, now a track, along the cliff top. Opposite number 79 Rosedale Lane are wooden gates leading to a viewing table giving information about Port Mulgrave, including a diagrammatic reconstruction of what its harbour would have looked like in 1911. From here you may decide to follow the path down the cliff and walk on the small remaining pier, before climbing back to this spot.

Continue along road in the same direction – signposted to the Ship Inn, behind the old ironstone miners cottages and past the telephone box. Carry straight on along Rosedale Lane to the Ship Inn.

Beyond the Ship Inn, walk to the end of the road at the churchyard of St Hilda's, Hinderwell. Turn left, walk to the T-junction and cross the main road to the village school. Walk down the lane to the right of the school and straight up the footpath to the centre of the row of cottages facing you. Turn right along the front of the cottages and left alongside no 33, Cosy Cottage.

The footpath takes a sharp right to emerge in a farmyard, straight across which, the quite narrow, but clear, path leads ahead with a hedge on the right, horse paddock and small caravan site to the left.

Reaching a small kissing gate, pass through and onto a wider track at a right angle bend. Carry straight ahead – there is a red house on the left – and up to the farm gate. Here, the main track (Back Lane Track) bends suddenly left but you carry straight on into the field – there is a stile beside the gate.

The path is a reserved grass strip to the side of the field, and at the corner are a gate and stile waymarked straight down the grass slope to another stile at the bottom, leading into woodland.

Cross the stile into the woods and follow the clearly trodden path down to the right, into the valley of Dales Beck and on to a series of steps down to the metal footbridge. Climb the steps straight ahead to the woodland edge and turn right into the field. Walk along the edge of the wood to the corner of the field where a gap leads back into the wood. Turn left, up hill just a few yards, and then keep on the well-trodden path all the way through the trees to a waymarked arrow at a gap in a barbed wire fence.

Pass through the gap, joining the track at a distinct corner. Turn right and walk on, finding a waymarker arrow pointing down to a wooden stile and footbridge. Walk up the other side and through a little clearing, until the path emerges from the woodland into pasture. Veer right along the grass path towards the telegraph pole. At this waymarked pole, cross the stile into the trees and follow the path up and round to the left emerging at a set of wooden steps rising to a stile over the railings of Hinderwell Lane roadside.

Turning left onto Hinderwell Lane follow the path along the other side to the public footpath sign on the right. Turn right onto this clear track and pass the concrete stile where there is a fork in the track. Take the left fork (bearing left rather than turning sharp left) and walk alongside the wire fence to a metal gate with a wooden stile next to it.

Proceed along the left edge of field to the corner and follow the hedge around the corner for a few yards to the stile in a gap in the hedge on the left. Crossing it, follow alongside the wire fence and old hedgerow to the right. Straight ahead is a modern farmhouse and over to the right a ruin – Cliff Farm.

Reaching the corner of the field cross the stile and turn left down the lane in front of the modern house ("Greenacres") to the end of the lane.

Take the public footpath indicated on the right and past some allotment gardens where it divides. Take the left-hand fork, uphill at first, emerging into the car park at Staithes cliff top.

To return to the Royal George, walk over to the far side of the car park and turn right along the road and down the hill into the old village.

Walk 16: Runswick Bay

Route: Runswick Bay – High Cliff – Kettleness – Tellgreen Hill – Overdale Farm – Fox and Hounds, Goldsborough – High Cliff – Runswick Bay.

Distance: 7 miles

Map: O.S. Outdoor Leisure 27, North York Moors Eastern Area (NE Sheet)

Start: Runswick Bay (car park) (Grid reference 809161)

Access: Runswick Bay lies at the foot of the cliffs, $1^1/_2$ miles south east of Hinderwell, off the A174 Whitby to Guisborough road. Tees bus service 256 from Whitby, Guisborough and Middlesbrough will take you to Runswick Bank Top, from which you can walk down the signposted road to the car park which I have made the starting point of this walk.

Unusually, the recommended pub is half-way round, at Goldsborough, but I think that this adds to the enjoyment of this particular coastal walk.

Runswick Bay

The pretty little village nestles against the cliff foot at the end of a stretch of sand curving south towards Kettleness. It is a very English small, seaside place in summer. Narrow alleyways and staircases lead between its tangle of buildings lending a real air of old world charm.

A line of traditional fishing boats "cobles" is to be seen along the shore. Cobles (pronounced 'cobbles') are the traditional design of boat used by North Yorkshire fisherfolk for centuries and are believed to follow an original Viking pattern. A rail-mounted winch higher on the cliff allows the cobles to be raised away from the rapidly advancing tide.

Runswick Bay

Goldsborough

This tiny agricultural hamlet lies just half a mile inland from the cliffs and has a longer history than you might imagine. It dates from the Romans who built a signal station on the hill top between here and Kettleness. This is another tiny community which you pass through on this walk; it had to be rebuilt after the entire village slid into the sea in 1829.

Fox and Hounds, Goldsborough (0947 83372)

A lovely little pub. Stone-built with a tiled roof in the smallest of villages, only a couple of fields inland from the cliffs, the Fox and Hounds has been a pub for 450 years. Tetleys is served nowadays, alongside Theakstons, in this free house. There are bar meals and sandwiches lunchtime and evening. There is a beer garden and children are welcome. Inside are two cosy, low ceilinged and beamed rooms and a hatch style bar off the long passage. Opening hours are 11.30am to 3pm and from 6pm to 11pm. On Sundays they change to 12noon to 2pm and 7pm to 11pm.

The Walk

From the car park in Runswick Bay, walk down the lifeboat slipway onto the beach. Turn right and walk along the beach past the beach chalets on your right. If the tide is in, follow the path along the base of the sea banks beyond the sea wall and onto the storm beach. When the cliff on your right becomes rock, you need to walk in an inland direction up the first stream-cut gorge.

For the first few yards, the path is the rock terrace of this stream, but you soon reach a footbridge waymarked with the acorn symbol of the Cleveland Way. Cross this bridge and begin the ascent up the cut steps of the path.

At the cliff top the grass path leads you round to the right. Ignore the wooden stile on your right as you come to the first field and press straight on along the cliff-top path enjoying the views of the wonderful coastal scenery here, and, behind you, over to idyllically-set Runswick Bay. It will be some time before you reach and cross the first of three wooden stiles into a succession of fields with a wire fence to your left separating you from the cliff edge.

After the path has dipped down and risen on the other side of one gulley, you will come across a second. Here, you need to walk 50 yards or so inland to a Cleveland Way marker post directing you left, over a wooden stile and onto a farm track. This is Kettleness Farm.

Entering the farmyard, bear left, as guided by the waymarker sign, and emerge from the yard into Kettleness hamlet itself. Opposite the cottages, a Cleveland Way marker directs you leftward, away from the surfaced minor road and onto the cliff-top path. A further waymark arrow guides you through a gap beside a gate next to a cliff top seat.

The Cleveland Way at this point is along a farm access track, but after you cross a wooden stile into a field it soon reduces in width again. There is now a dry stone wall on your left.

Cross the first of two further stiles and follow the cliff top wire fence on your left. The path then joins the line of the old dismantled railway. Continue heading south to the next stile and cross this into a field.

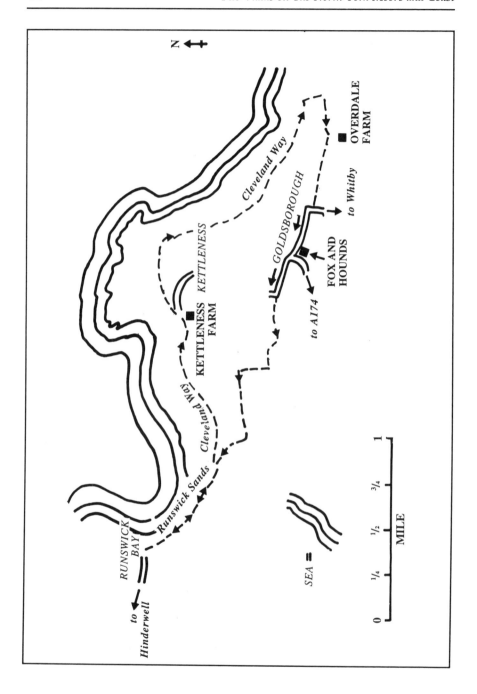

Follow the fence on your left and cross stiles into further fields, enjoying more of the cliff views which are such a feature of this walk, until you come to a Cleveland Way signpost at a fork.

At this sign, cross the stile and turn sharp right alongside the wire fence, heading inland in the direction of Lythe. At the first field boundary you reach, turn right through the gateway, following the waymark arrow.

Follow the track along the right-hand side of the field beside a low hedge. Cross the stile into the next field and leave the farm track where it bends left about half-way across the field. Press straight on, initially following the line of the hedge on your right until you reach a gate at which there are two waymark arrows.

Follow the straight ahead option, through the gate, along the farm track, with the hedgerow still to your right, until you reach the minor road, Goldsborough Lane. Turn right along the road and then sharp left around the bend, following the lane into Goldsborough village.

The Fox and Hounds is the first building in the village on your left and is well worth calling into for mid-walk refreshment.

Continue along the lane to the junction and walk straight on in the direction of Kettleness until you reach a distinct right-hand bend. Here you head straight onto a track, away from the road through a gateway. This is a signposted public footpath.

Cross the first stile you reach onto the obvious farm track beyond, but head for the wooden stile 20 yards to the right of the gateway on the far side of the field.

This waymarked stile leads us across into a further pasture. Follow the line of the hedge on your left to the waymark arrow in the field corner. Turn right along the side of the field, heading towards the sea. In the next corner is a wooden stile which you cross into the next field.

Walk along the field edge, hedge on your right, and cross the stile in the corner. Walk along the edge of the next field, a wire fence now on your right, and across its stile. You will now find the hedgerow and fence line to your left. At the following corner there are waymarks on the stile to both left and right. Turn right towards the sea, and a gate where there is a stile to cross, before proceeding straight ahead, keeping the wire fence and hedge on the right.

There is a low step over the fence you reach leading into a short green lane, between two hedges, and across a stile and stone bridge over the dismantled railway line. Following the path as it veers left across the field, you will cross a stile and meet the cliff-top path again at High Cliff.

Turn left and follow the path back down to the beach. Carry on along to the sea wall at Runswick Bay. If the tide is out you can walk along the beach into the village, but if it is in, you will need to take the path along the base of the sea banks.

Walk 17: Hutton Rudby

Route: The King's Head – North End – Hutton Bridge – Skutterskelfe Park – Sexhow Hall – Sexhow Grange – Moor House – River Leven – Hutton Bridge – Hutton Rudby.

Distance: 5 miles

Map: O.S. Outdoor Leisure 26, North York Moors Western Area (NW Sheet)

Start: The King's Head (Grid reference 468064)

Access: Hutton Rudby lies on the minor road between the Crathorne exit of the A19 (3 miles to the west) and the market town of Stokesley, 4 miles to the east. For drivers coming from the south, the village is 3 miles north from the A172 Cleveland Tontine to Stokesley road, turning off opposite Swainby village.

The village is served by two bus routes. Tees services 90, from Middlesbrough, Stokesley and Northallerton, and 270 from Stockton, Middlesbrough, Yarm and Stokesley. The latter operates seven days a week, the former on Mondays to Saturdays.

The King's Head (0642 700342)

Dating from at least 1830, this small, locals' village pub is a friendly and welcoming house at the top end of the village green, by the Post Office. Inside there is a beamed and cosy bar-lounge with two real fires and four real ales on sale. Resident beers are Camerons Strongarm and Tetley Bitter, with the other two pumps rotating around Castle Eden, Camerons Bitter, Flowers and Burton Ale.

Food includes Sunday lunch (from 12-2pm) and, during the week, a varied menu in the bistro which is open for bookings only. Bar snacks are available most evenings, as are pizzas to eat-in or take-away. In summer there are Saturday evening barbecues on the patio at the rear.

There is a darts room and dominoes are available. Quiz night is Tuesday.

The King's Head is open from 6.30pm to 11.00pm (7pm to 10.30pm on Sundays) and on week-end lunchtimes from 12 noon until 3pm on Saturdays and 2pm on Sundays. The pub also opens its door for Bank Holiday lunch-times.

The King's Head

Hutton Rudby

Hutton Rudby stands high above the River Leven, on its southern bank. Pretty 18th-century cottages surround the delightful tree-planted village green and include various architectural features of interest – Yorkshire sliding light windows, little spinners' or weavers' windows in some, and a curious arrangement of doors and chimneys.

The front doors of several cottages were formerly access tunnels between pairs of cottages so that they appear quirkily offset from the houses they serve. Similarly, chimneys frequently emerge from the roof of the next door cottage.

On the opposite bank of the Leven stands 13th century All Saints Church, in the dip by Hutton Bridge. Properly, this is in Rudby rather than Hutton Rudby, the river acting as the dividing line between the two.

Wandering around the attractive green, and venturing down the offshoot North End, at the beginning of this walk, it may strike you that, even ignoring more modern housing around the village fringe, Hutton is quite large for a country village of two centuries past. This is due to its industrial heritage as a textile manufacturing settlement, based initially on cottage industry and later at the mill by Hutton Bridge.

The Mill

Closed down in 1908, though not pulled down for some years afterwards, Hutton Mill produced linen and sailcloth, originally using water power from the Leven and flax from the Moors, and later converted to steam operation. Many cottages in Hutton would have housed mill workers.

Cholera

In the early 19th century cholera was a scourge of unknown origin and terrible power when it struck, and it certainly caused fear among the villagers of Hutton Rudby, many of whom fled from the epidemic. Those less fortunate were buried, it is thought, in a common grave marked only by the low grassy mound at the rear of the church.

The Walk

With your back to the King's Head, turn right along the street to the Post Office and right again down North End. As you turn the corner you will see a double fronted cottage facing you.

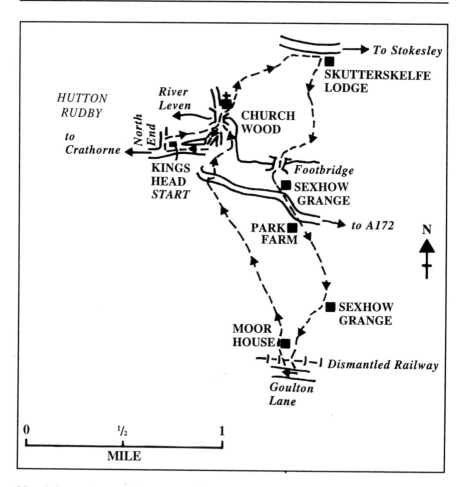

Head down the road to pass this cottage on your right, to see the pretty cottages of this quiet corner of the village better. Look out for the little "weavers' windows" still to be seen in some.

Opposite the tree which has a seat below it is a waymarked footpath along the side of a cottage. Follow this path to a stile and cross into a field. Walk straight across to the next stile and, crossing it, continue along the bank-side, high above the River Leven.

When the way divides, turn left down a flight of steps and then along a stony track to a metal gate. Cross the adjacent stile into the field beyond, flat because it was the site of the former mill.

Emerge from the field onto the road and cross the bridge to the church. Pass through the lych gate into All Saints churchyard and head left to go behind the church. Keeping close by the wall of the church, you will notice a grassy mound to your left which is reputedly the common grave of the victims of the cholera epidemic.

Make your way back round the church and follow the path across the modern cemetery to a gap in the fence. Cross the footbridge here and go into Church Wood. Take the path leading up the slope to your left and bear left again, making your way uphill to the top of the woods.

Cross the stile and walk along the edge of the field to your left, keeping the fence on your left. Reaching the white railings of a footbridge, turn right and head along the path across the field to a stile.

Over this stile, you come to another field and then another, again by means of a stile in the hedge. The next stile is just to the left of the top corner of this new field. Cross it, a strip of grassland, and another stile from which Roseberry Topping is visible.

Continue along the grass path to a gravel drive leading to the minor road via a gate in a brick wall. Turn right along the wall and walk along the grass strip towards the lodge house at the bottom of the slope. Turn right here along a metal estate-style rail fence, keeping it on your left. Ignore a stile on your left and keep going to a stile which you cross into a large field and follow the path directly across the field.

At the corner, turn right towards a gate and brick barn beyond. The path has been diverted and may appear to take a slightly different course from that on your O.S. map. Through the gate, turn left and down the bank, hedge on your left towards the River Leven. Cross the metal footbridge over the river and follow the track on the other side, up and around to the farm at Sexhow Hall.

Going through the gate, walk up to the minor road. Turn left along the minor road, and walk along it to Sexhow Park Farm. Pass through the gate to the left of the farm buildings and then through two more gates to continue along the farm track to Sexhow Grange.

On your right you will see a green metal gate, and to the left of it a gap takes you through onto the footpath. After a few yards, you will find yourself walking between two lines of wire fence. This brings you down into a wooded glade by a stream. Follow the path up and into a field. Turn right, skirting the edge of the field, with the wooded beck to your right. Continue until you come onto a track leading from the small caravan site you have just past. Passing between the stone bridge supports which used to carry the old railway from Stokesley, come onto the minor road, Goulton Lane.

Turn right along the lane across the bridge with white railings and then right again along the public footpath which is indicated right through a gap in the hedge. Go down to the stile and cross it to climb some wooden steps to another stile on the line of the old railway.

Coming into a grass field, you can see Moor House straight in front. At Moor House, the footpath goes left and around the back to a stile by a metal gate. Instead of crossing this stile, turn left and walk along with the wire fence on your right.

You can now see Hutton Rudby ahead in the distance. Keep following the wire fence across three fields. Cross the waymarked stile down into a shaded wood and cross the stream by means of the footbridge. Climb straight up the far bank and walk on alongside the hedge on your left until you cross another two stiles. Continue along the fence to your left until you cross a second footbridge, reached by a stile just to the left of the field corner.

The path rises on the other side to take you over the next pasture field and so onto a lane by the side of a large garage with red doors. Turn right and walk down and around the corner to a footpath on your left, leading via a kissing gate into the trees. Follow this path down to and then alongside the River Leven, crossing a stile on the way, until you arrive at the steps up to Hutton Bridge. From the top of the steps, carry straight on up the road to the village green. Turn right and make your way up to the King's Head at the far end of the green.

Walk 18: Beck Hole

Route: Beck Hole – Mallyan Spout Waterfall – St Mary's Church – Two
Howes – St Mary's Church – Moorgates – Sadler House – Goathland –
Rail Trail – Beck Hole

Distance: $7^1/_4$ miles

Map: O.S. Outdoor Leisure 27, North York Moors Eastern Area (NE
Sheet)

Start: Birch Hall Inn (Grid reference 823022)

Access: Beck Hole lies, as its name would suggest, deep in a stream
valley – that of the Eller Beck, a northward flowing tributary of the Esk,
joining the latter at Grosmont, some 2 miles walk north along the Rail
Trail which follows the line of a dismantled railway from Grosmont to
Goathland. The southern section of the Rail Trail forms a part of this
walk.

By public transport, you can reach the tiny hamlet of Beck Hole by
means of the privately-run North York Moors Railway from Pickering or
Grosmont (where it connects with the BR Middlesbrough to Whitby
service). You can either walk along the Rail Trail south from Grosmont,
or alight at Goathland and join this walk there.

There are buses to Goathland, though not Beck Hole. Tees service 128
from Whitby (0947 602146) and Yorkshire Coastliner 840/842 from
Leeds, York, Malton, Pickering or Whitby (0653 692556) will get you
there, but check times in advance.

Birch Hall Inn (0947 86245)

This exceptional little pub sells Theakstons Ales (Best Bitter, XB and
Mild) and dates back to at least the dawn of the 18th century; it has
remained unchanged in layout for 80 years.

It is split into three self-contained public rooms. To the left, as you face the inn, there is a doorway with "Public Entrance" written above it. Through this door you come to the sitting room bar where service is through a hatch and time, like the hands of the pendulum clock, stands still. The walls of this very traditionally furnished room, with old wooden chairs, bench seats round the sides and an open fire, are covered with old photographs of village quoits teams, Beck Hole and the pub itself.

The Birch Hall Inn

Food is described as simple bar fare and consists of a choice between pork pie, hot or cold, with pickle, or a Beck Hole Butty – cheese, corned beef, or ham sandwiched within a wedge of wholemeal bread. Alternatively, there are scones and home-made cakes to enjoy with morning coffee or afternoon tea, during opening hours which are 11am to 11pm on summer weekdays and Saturdays. In winter, there is a closure between 3pm and 7.30 pm, and Sunday hours are 12 to 3pm and 7 to 10.30 pm.

There are two other doors at the front of the Birch Hall Inn. One is labelled "Shop", the other "Bar". This bar is a very small drinking area, just a couple of tables, fronting a conventional counter bar with pumps. It is the easiest place to buy drinks to take outside, if you are going to sit at one of the tables in front of the pub.

The little shop, as well as selling postcards and ice creams, is a treasure trove of by-gone confectionery – a midget gem of its own, so to speak. There are also aniseed balls, "fried eggs", Pontefract cakes, liquorice sticks, and just about anything else you can remember from the corner shops of childhood.

There is also a terrace garden offering lovely views over the Eller Beck valley, and even the pub sign has its own little slice of history. Painted on metal, this picture of Eller Beck is the work of one Algernon Newton, member of the Royal Academy no less, and is carefully preserved behind glass.

Beck Hole

The Birch Hall Inn is the main building of this tiny hamlet. It is sited at a bridging point of the Eller Beck, just below the Thomason Foss waterfall, and just upstream of its confluence with West Beck to form the muddily-named Murk Esk. In the mid-19th century iron mining briefly flourished here, but that is long gone and idyllic rural peace pervades the Beck Hole of today.

Goathland

A sprawling moorland settlement, Goathland stretches out over nearly a mile from the church of St Mary to the North York Moors railway. It is a very open settlement in plan, and the grassy spaces are kept short by the freely wandering sheep.

The origins of the name are uncertain, though St Mary's Hermitage, fore-runner of the present church, was established in Godeland ("God's Land") in the twelfth century. However, a pre-Christian origin as a Scandinavian Goda's or Goth's settlement is equally plausible.

The most famous natural attraction of Goathland is undoubtedly the Mallyan Spout, a beautiful and slender cascade of some 70 feet of sparkling water which pours down to West Beck from the steep and wooded left bank.

The Walk

Facing the front of the Birch Hall Inn, head right towards the hill, but turn instead immediately right through a wooden gate, guided by a public bridleway sign. Walking along with a hedgerow to your left and dry stone wall to your right, you will come to a second gate.

Pass through this gate and approach a pair of waymark posts. Take the direction indicated by a yellow arrow towards Goathland and pass the stone Honeysuckle Cottage on your left as you come near to Incline Cottage.

Opposite the fenced garden of Incline Cottage is a wooden kissing gate through which you should pass. This is next to a five-bar gate which has a sign saying "To the Mallyan". Beyond, walk along the path, keeping the stream, West Beck, on your right.

Go through a second kissing gate and walk alongside the wire fence which now separates the path from the stream. Ascend a flight of cut steps and then continue to follow the fence on your right. Go through more kissing gates, down and across some wooden boards, until you come to a green bench by a waymarker pointing left to Goathland.

Carry straight on past this sign and you will come unmistakably to the Mallyan Spout waterfall on your left. Turn round and walk back to the waymark post you passed earlier. Turn right towards Goathland, walking through trees to a set of steps with a wooden hand-rail. Beyond the top of these, the path brings you along the side of the Mallyan Spout Hotel to St Mary's Church opposite.

Head right to the road junction and, to make the ascent to Two Howes, take the right-hand fork which is signposted to Egton Bridge. Having done so, you will pass by a curiously walled-in tree on your left and should then follow the waymarked public bridleway – a grass track

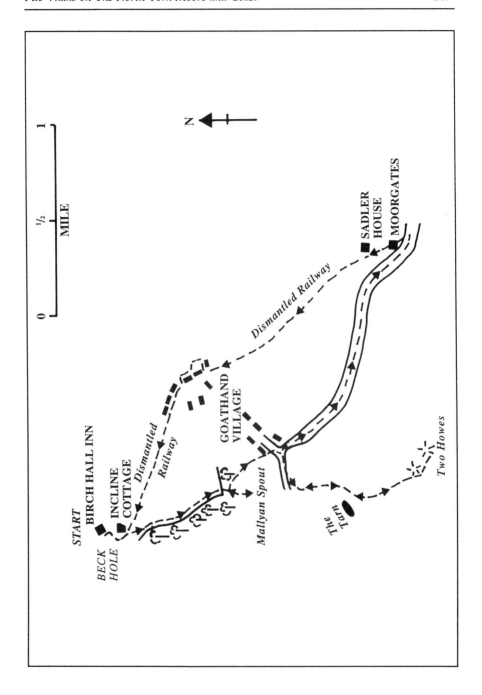

between the ferns of the now open moor.

As the slope levels out at a more open space, directly opposite a detached and red-roofed villa, the way divides. Fork left here and follow the bridle path as it curves right beside a small lake – The Tarn.

Above the tarn are fine, open views in all directions from the point where the bridle path bends left and passes a low cairn. Keep following the path across the open heather moor with lush green Wheeldale visible over to your right. A series of further low cairns marks the way to the first of the two larger cairns of Two Howes, 252m above sea level.

Although a bridleway is shown on the O.S. map leading south to meet another on Two Howes Rigg which would lead in turn to the road above Moorgates, this is not evident on the ground. Accordingly, you need to descend the way you have come, back to the road junction by St Mary's Church, and turn right along the road in the direction of Pickering.

Walk alongside this unfenced minor road until you come to Moorgates. Turn left by the house, through a signposted kissing gate, along the line of the old railway.

Passing Sadler House farm on your right, you go through another kissing gate and continue along the now grassy track of the dismantled railway. Keep going until you come to a waymark sign at a route crossing.

Follow the direction "Goathland", and the path will bring you to that village, emerging opposite a garage. Turn right along the road and then left by the public footpath sign, through a gateway onto the Mill Green Way.

Mill Green Way bends left and right and leads you to another minor road. Turn left and then immediately right, through a kissing gate, following the waymarked Rail Trail.

Descend the incline along this gravelly track, until you arrive back at appropriately named Incline Cottage. Carry on to the two waymarkers, and turn right through the wooden gate and along the lane to Beck Hole and the Birch Hall Inn.

Mallyan Spout

Walk 19: Osmotherley

Route: Osmotherley – Chapel Wood Farm – Black Share – Coldbeck Reservoir – Chequers – White House Farm – Osmotherley

Distance: $6^1/_2$ miles

Map: O.S. Outdoor Leisure 26, North York Moors Western Area (SW Sheet)

Start: The Golden Lion, Osmotherley (Grid reference 456973)

Access: Osmotherley lies 1 mile east of the A19 trunk road's junction with the A684 to Northallerton where there is a main-line railway station. The village can be reached by bus from Northallerton and Stokesley (Tees services 90 and 90A, Mondays to Saturdays); from Northallerton, on Wednesdays only, by Atkinson's Coaches (060982-222); and from Northallerton and Stockton by the once a week Tees service 296 on Saturdays only, leaving Northallerton at 10.12 and Stockton at 16.02.

The Golden Lion (060 983 526)

Base pub of the Lyke Wake Walk, the sandstone-built Golden Lion lies beside the market cross of Osmotherley with a couple of rustic benches outside for customers' use.

Inside the pub has a small and cosy bar to the left and dining area to the right. It has been refurbished, but retains the proportions and feel of a country village pub. Bar meals are well known locally and popular enough to justify booking a table at busy periods, especially in summer or in the run-up to Christmas.

On offer are John Smith's Magnet and Bitter and Courage Directors, from 11am to 3pm and 6pm to 11pm.

The Golden Lion

The Three Tuns (060 983 301)

An early 17th century inn, previously known locally as the Mousehole, the Three Tuns is an alternative to the Golden Lion, and just across the street from it, with a high local reputation for its food. It has a restaurant, as well as two small, low ceilinged bar rooms. There is an old, walled beer garden to the rear. Real ales served are Theakstons XB, Best Bitter and Old Peculier, as well as Youngers Scotch Bitter and No.3. Bar and restaurant meals are freshly prepared to order using fresh fish and local game and meat. Bed and breakfast, including en-suite accommodation, is available. Opening hours are 12 noon to 3.30pm and 7pm to 11 pm.

Osmotherley

Osmotherley is well known nationally as the western end of the 40 miles in a day challenge of the Lyke Wake Walk to Ravenscar on the coast.

A lovely green village, with a medieval church and unusual Viking tomb, it boasts three stone built pubs, in sight of each other around the butter cross, from which John Wesley spoke. Beside the cross stands a low stone table, which, it is claimed may be an old market stall.

Mount Grace Priory

Mount Grace Priory is the best preserved Carthusian monastery in the country and dates from the 14th century. Prior to abolition by Henry VIII, the monks of Mount Grace led solitary lives of prayer, each having his own cell, so that the monastery's plan is most unusual.

An English Heritage property, Mount Grace Priory is open from 10am to 4pm in October to March, every day except Monday and from 10am to 6pm from April to September. Admission charges at the time of writing were £1.80 for adults, £1.40 concessions and 90p for children.

Mount Grace Priory

Chequers (060 983 291)

A former droving inn, Chequers is now a farm with shop and tea room, situated $1^1/_2$ miles east of Osmotherley, along the route of this walk. The tea room is open 7 days a week in summer, and weekends during the rest of the year, although if the weather is sunny, Chequers may be open during the week in autumn and spring. It is well worth a stop, offering an unexpected chance for refreshment and fine views west over the Vale of Mowbray. There is game for sale here, as well as free range eggs and home-made preserves.

The Walk

With your back to the Golden Lion turn left towards the market cross and left again up the hill past the Coffee Pot cafe. Continue up past the Top Shop and the public footpath sign at Grant Close.

Further uphill, turn left into Ruebury Lane, which is waymarked "Cleveland Way, Scarth Nick $2^1/_2$ miles". Continue along the track past the last of the houses, to a fork where you bear left rather than walking up the hill to the signposted Lady Chapel – an early 16th century addition to Carthusian Mount Grace Priory.

The path leads down past Chapel Wood Farm on the left. From here it is possible to walk the three-quarters of a mile down to Mount Grace Priory.

Passing Chapel Wood Farm on your left, go through the waymarked kissing gate and take the lower track through two pasture fields. From here there are extensive views across the Vale of York, westward to the Pennines on the horizon. At the far boundary of the second field is a kissing gate beyond which the track divides.

Branch off to the right, heading uphill through South Wood following the waymarked Cleveland Way. Emerging from the trees onto more open moorland, there is a division of the paths. Take the right hand, minor, fork. Follow this path round through heather and fern until you reach a gate in a dry-stone wall.

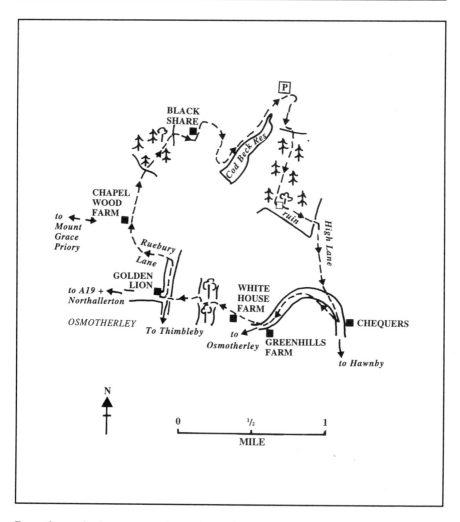

Pass through the gate and continue, keeping the dry stone wall on your left and enjoying views over the Vale of York and Ingleby and Scarth Wood Moors. Reaching another gate, pass through it and turn left along the surfaced minor road past the stone buildings of Black Share before turning right along a dry stone wall, through a gate, following the footpath sign to Quarry Gate.

Proceed down the grassy slope, keeping the dry stone wall on your right. At the bottom, cross a wooden stile and follow the winding path down through ferns to a flatter stretch where there are evenly spaced trees. The path heads through these trees, veering away from the dry stone wall which is now on your left.

Walking along through the trees, Coldbeck Reservoir is clearly visible down to the left. A well-trodden path descends gently, parallel to the reservoir until taking a left down to the road between a pair of dry stone walls. Turn left along Quarry Lane, and walk along with the reservoir on your right, across the cattle grid onto the National Trust land of Scarth Wood Moor.

At the northern end of the reservoir the trees end, and there is a small car park on the more open ground. Turn right across the car park and onto the clear footpath through the heather beyond. Keeping to the right, the path leads you down to stepping stones and over the stream.

On the other side, the path initially follows the line of a wire fence on the right. This soon turns away and the path continues straight ahead, before curving left, keeping the dry stone wall on the right, until you reach a stile.

Cross the stile over the wall and onto a grassy path. Carry straight ahead through the plantation until you reach a right angle in a forest track. Continue straight ahead, joining the track, and then keeping straight ahead again at the following cross-roads of forest tracks.

As the edge of the plantation is evident ahead, there is a ruin on your left. Turn left here, onto the path which runs along the far side of the ruin, keeping the remains on your left, and, now among deciduous trees, continue straight ahead.

Emerging from the forest via a stile over a wire fence, onto High Lane track, turn right and carry on until the track joins the minor road at Solomon's Temple. Keep going straight ahead alongside the road to Chequers.

From Chequers, the path descending to Osmotherley, is clearly visible, though not initially waymarked and you will need to cross the minor road to join it and follow it until it rejoins the minor road further downhill.

Turn left and walk along the road past Trenholm House on the right and Greenhills Farm on the left, down to the cattle grid. A few yards past this grid, follow the public footpath sign right, over a stile, into a field. Follow the hedge to your right to the other side where you pass between two standing stones onto a grass track. Cross this track and pass between a similar pair of stones, waymarked "Cleveland Way".

The track, on your right, leads you down towards farm buildings – White House Farm. Here the path veers right, following a sign on a telegraph pole, and brings you to the first of two stiles. Crossing these, and a track cutting across the route, the path leads into woods and down wood-edged steps onto a footbridge crossing Middlestye Beck.

Follow the clearly defined path up the far bank and emerge from the woods into a grass field. Cross the middle of the field to a gate and over its adjacent stile into a second field at the far side of which are two standing stones beside a track. Pass between the stones onto the waymarked path alongside a hedge on your left. Follow this path through further pairs of stones as far as the road.

Cross the road and follow the signed Cleveland Way down a narrow gap and onto Osmotherley's main street. The Golden Lion is on the opposite side.

Walk 20: Nether Silton

Route: Nether Silton – Hunter's Hill – Black Hill – Hambleton Street – Nab Farm – Nether Silton

Distance: 8 miles

Map: O.S. Outdoor Leisure 26, North York Moors Western Area (SW Sheet)

Start: The Gold Cup Inn (Grid reference 454923)

Access: The village of Nether Silton is situated at the foot of the Hambleton Hills, 2 miles to the east of the A19 trunk road, from which it is clearly signposted just north of Leake Church which is about 5 miles north of Thirsk.

A tiny settlement, Nether Silton, like its neighbour Over Silton, is not directly accessible by public transport. It is possible to reach Osmotherley by bus (see Walk 19), and you could walk along Oakdale from there to join this walk at Hambleton End, but this would involve an extra $2^1/_2$ miles each way.

The Gold Cup Inn (060983 416)

The pub's name commemorates one of the country's first horse races – the four-mile "His Majesty's Gold Cup", first run at Hambleton, at the top of Sutton Bank, in 1715. In 1740, only Hambleton and Newmarket were legally allowed flat racing, which continued on the Moors course until 1775, when the race, by now the "Hambleton 100 Guineas", was transferred to York.

Today's Gold Cup Inn maintains the link with the old course by offering Hambleton Ale, as well as John Smith's. From Monday to Friday, the pub is open evenings only, from 7 to 11pm. On Saturdays and Bank Holidays an 11.30am to 2.30pm lunchtime session is added. Sunday opening is 12 noon to 3pm and 7pm to 10.30 pm. Restaurant meals are available on Tuesday evenings through to Saturday from 7.30pm to 9.30pm, sandwiches at lunchtimes, and Sunday lunch, in the restaurant, from 12.30 to 2.00pm. The restaurant is entirely No Smoking.

Nether Silton

Like its near neighbour Over Silton, the village is a very small community indeed. Pub apart, there are no other services remaining for its handful of stone cottages scattered around the green, so it is a real haven of peace and tranquillity.

Adders

These snakes, one of only three species native to Britain, are timid creatures and, though they are poisonous, will not harm you if you leave them alone. You may chance to see an adder basking in the sun on the descent from the Hambleton Drove Road to Nab Hill Farm, so keep an eye out for the distinctive zig-zag marking.

The Drove Road – Hambleton Street

Part of the ancient droving route between Scotland and East Anglia, Hambleton Street parallels the tolled turnpike of the Great North Road in the vale below. It was used by drovers from Scotland to drive their cattle and sheep to market and to the annual fairs in York and Malton. The section of the Drove Road included in this walk is also part of the Cleveland Way and affords tremendous views across the Vale of Mowbray to the distant Pennines.

The Walk

From the Gold Cup, turn left onto the street of Nether Silton and pass the school before turning left down Kirk Ings Lane, following the signpost pointing the way to Over Silton.

At the cottages you reach on your right, turn right along the track beside the "No Through Road" sign. Follow this track , initially uphill and then along Moor Lane, passing Moor House on your right and Hunter's Hill Farm on your left, ignoring a waymarked footpath to your right. Carry

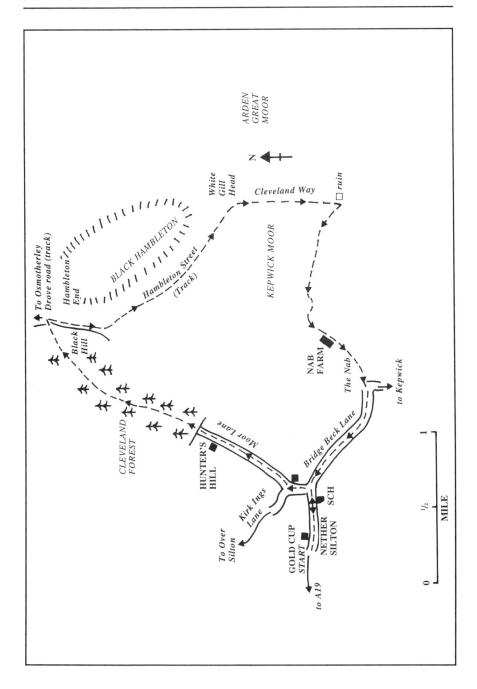

on along Moor Lane into the woodlands of Cleveland Forest, passing Silton Picnic Place. Press straight on, ignoring tracks to left and right, and keep going until you pass through a large wooden gate. Uphill from the gate, you will pass a turkey farm on your left and come to a fork. Keep to the main Moor Lane – the leftward fork.

When the lane levels out, it takes you round a right hand bend to a green forest track, a firebreak, which cuts across your way. Carry straight on and round a right-hand bend to a fork. At this fork, leave the main track and bear right along the grassy way which will bring you to a gate, through which you reach the open moor.

You find yourself on the rough track that is Hambleton Street – the old drove road. Turn right along it with the forest's dry stone wall boundary on your right. Climbing this track, it is worth looking back for extensive views over to the summits of the Cleveland Hills, Chequers (see Walk 19), Osmotherley and the Vale of York.

On reaching a defined corner in the track, at White Gill Head, there is a Cleveland Way marker-post. Follow the Cleveland Way around to your right. At a waymarked gate across Hambleton Street, you should pass through to find a short section with dry stone walls on either side. Just before the end of this section, a few yards in front of a dry stone wall which half cuts across the lane, turn right opposite a ruin.

This turn takes you through a wooden gate inscribed "Beware Adders". Proceed along the grass path, with a dry stone wall on your left, down the slope. Continue along the path when the wall becomes a wire fence, and round a left-hand bend to come to a wooden gate set in a dry stone wall. Go through the gate and walk down the slope to join the track at the bottom. Turn right onto this farm track and follow it across the stream, up and around to the left to Nab Farm.

At Nab Farm, pass through a pair of gates alongside a cow byre. Then continue straight ahead down the lane to reach the cattle grid at the Nab. Keep following the main track, in the same direction, to a second cattle grid at the bend of a minor road.

Turn right here and walk along the road (Bridge Beck Lane). Rounding a 90 degree right-hand bend, continue along the lane and, passing the school, return to Nether Silton village.

Walk 21: Ruswarp

Route: Ruswarp – Briggswath – Sleights – Northdale House – Hagg House – Esk Valley Railway – Sneaton Lane – Ruswarp

Distance: 4 miles

Map: O.S. Outdoor Leisure 27, North York Moors Eastern Area (NE Sheet)

Start: The Bridge Inn (Grid reference 889092)

Access: Ruswarp village stands at a bridging point of the River Esk, where the B1410 and B1416 roads converge, 2 miles drive inland from Whitby. On British Rail's Esk Valley line, Ruswarp is accessible by train from Whitby and Middlesbrough. Bus travellers can easily reach Ruswarp from Whitby using local Tees Clipper services C4, C5 and C6 or Tees & District's 128 Whitby to Goathland bus. In addition, Yorkshire Coastliner runs some services on its 840/842 routes from Pickering, Malton, York and Leeds which call at Ruswarp. Telephone them on 0653 692556 for up to date details of timings.

The Bridge Inn (0947 602780)

The Bridge Inn is, as its name suggests, right by the bridge at Ruswarp, on the north bank of the Esk opposite the local rail station. Beamed and wood-panelled, with a cosy bar-room warmed by a real fire and a separate dining room, it has a lovely riverside beer garden.

It is a traditional locals' pub with beams, brasses and old photographs of Ruswarp and itself, including flood scenes, around the walls. Real ales are John Smith's Bitter and Magnet, as well as guest beers, and food consists of snacks and hot bar fare, as well as restaurant meals and Sunday lunch.

Opening is from 12 noon to 3pm and 6pm to 11pm in winter, 12 to 3pm and 7 to 11pm on Sundays. It is hoped to extend summer opening to 11am to 11pm, so telephone to check if it matters to you.

The Bridge Inn

Ruswarp

Prettily set in the lower Esk Valley, Ruswarp lies only a mile or two upstream of Whitby. Until the recent building of the new Esk Bridge, it was the lowest permanent bridging point of the river – in the sense that there is an opening road bridge at Whitby harbour. The attractive river bank is popular in summer and boats are offered for hire.

Sleights

A river crossing place since ancient times, Sleights bridge replaced the ford in 1190, but was swept away by floodwaters in 1720. Rebuilt that century, it was swept away again in 1930 and re-sited at its present slightly upstream location in 1937. From the bridge it is possible to see salmon leaping in season.

Ruswarp

The Walk

Emerging from the Bridge Inn, turn left and left again along the B1410 road which is signposted to Sleights and Pickering. Follow the road alongside the River Esk, passing a lock and weir on your left, as far as the hiring quay of Ruswarp Pleasure Boats. Opposite this jetty is Esk Leisure Centre's car park, from which the signposted public footpath sets off along a grass track, leading obliquely up the rise and over a pitch and put course.

Go through a small cutting ahead of you, and curve round to the right to cut across the upper section of the pitch and put course and come to a waymarked stile taking you into an area of scrubland. Walk along the path ahead of you onto a farm track which leads you up the rise towards a gate through a hedgerow. To the left of the gate is a waymark arrow directing you to the left, over a stile and into a pasture field.

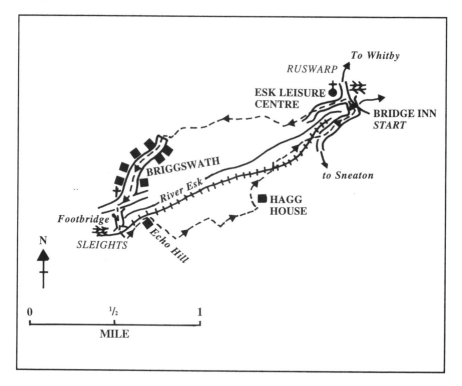

Follow the hedge on your right, around the edge of this pasture, to a further waymarked stile. Cross this into a rougher pasture field and you will now find that the hedgerow is to your left as you walk over to the next stile.

Crossing the next stile you emerge into a further field where the waymarking guides you left along the edge of the field, hedgerow on your left. Reaching the field corner, there is a magnificent view up the Esk Valley to enjoy as you turn right to walk now along the bottom edge of the field.

Having followed the field edge right around to the far end, find a public footpath marker at which to turn left through a gateway onto a track leading to a cul-de-sac of houses. Follow the road here around to your right until you come to a junction with a minor road where you should turn left downhill. Keep going until you come to the B1410 road again at the bottom of the hill in Briggswath, by the Wesleyan chapel.

Begin by turning right along the B-road, but then turn left to cross the blue metal footbridge over the Esk to Sleights village station. Cross the railway line and the road in front of you to head along Low Dale Lane. Here, you come to a public bridleway sign which directs you straight ahead where the road itself bends around left to Echo Hill.

Carry straight on and you will soon find yourself walking along the bank of a stream to your left, and, following this around to the left, you will reach Beck Holme. At this point, a waymarker points your way left and across a footbridge. Cross this and walk along the edge of the village recreation field, past a stone barn and the pavilion to a set of white gates.

Pass through the gates and turn right and then immediately left on to the track up the hill. At the top of the rise you will see a waymarker ahead of you on a telegraph pole. This sends you right. Walk along the track to a metal gate and then through it. Continue along the green lane ahead of you, hedgerow now on your left, to a second metal gate taking you into a pasture field. Here a footpath waymarker signpost points your way straight ahead and slightly round to the right along the edge of the field, with a line of low trees on your right. From here are views down the Esk Valley to your left and up valley and over to Sleights on your right.

At the field corner, head left along the top edge of the field with quite a tall hedgerow on your right, until you come to the next field corner. Here you will find a waymarker post leading you straight on, but a slight stagger means that you continue along the way with the hedgerow now on your left.

So you come to a stile which you cross into the next field so that you continue along the bottom edge of the next field with the hedgerow on your left. Half-way across you will find the first of two waymarkers keeping you going along the edge of the field as it slightly bends right uphill.

From the top corner of this field, there is a marvellous view of the Esk Valley to digest, before following the waymarker left through a gateway. Immediately, you see Whitby Abbey straight ahead of you on the horizon. Carry straight along the field edge, with a wire fence on your left. A waymarker along your way keeps you going in the correct direction, and from this point you can see the spire of Ruswarp's church.

At the field corner, cross the stile and then dip down to a further waymarker in the gulley bottom, before climbing the other side to another stile. Across the stile, continue straight on over the brow of the field and follow the track to the farm buildings of Hagg House ahead.

By these buildings a footpath sign indicates your way left across the stile, and you continue down with the hedgerow on your left until a wire fence runs across your way. To the right, a stile takes you over the fence and enables you to carry on downhill.

Walking along a grass path now, you will have a wire fence on your right. This path takes you round to the right, the wire fence becoming a hedgerow, and down the slope towards the railway line.

Cross the stile at the slope foot and continue through two metal gates as you cross the railway. Then turn right along the track which runs parallel to the rails until you come to a further metal gate. Pass through the gate and carry on to white gates which lead you to re-cross the railway. Continue up the track on the other side, ignoring a road leading off to a public footpath sign on your right, and emerge onto the B1416 road at a bend.

Turn left and walk down the hill into Ruswarp, crossing the bridge to return to the Bridge Inn.

Walk 22: Harome

Route: Harome – Hall Lane – Seamer Great Wood – Leysthorpe Lane – Seamer Little Wood – Sproxton Hall – Fish Farm – Harome

Distance: 7^1/$_2$ miles

Map: O.S. Outdoor Leisure 26, North York Moors Western Area (SW Sheet)

Start: The Star (Grid reference 646822)

Access: Harome is to be found 2 miles south-east of the A170, as you drive out of Helmsley towards Kirkbymoorside. The village may be reached by bus 6 days a week – Monday to Saturday. The Yorkshire Coastliner service number 94 runs three times a day between Helmsley and Malton, passing through Harome en route. For up to date timings, you can contact the bus company on 0653 692556.

The Star (0439 70397)

The Star is a fourteenth century, thatched, cruck-framed pub with a pretty beer garden, serving Theakston, Tetley and Timothy Taylor Landlord real ales. There are excellent home-prepared bar meals – "even our fruit pies are made with fruit from our own garden."

The entrance is via a stable door and takes you into a cosy, low-ceilinged bar, furnished substantially with old wood and decked out with a variety of rural paraphernalia arranged around the wood-panelled walls. There are magazines and books to browse through and a real fire at the far end.

Opening hours are 12 noon to 3pm and 7pm (6.30pm if you're lucky) until 11pm.

Harome

Harome is situated on the lowlands which lie along the southern edge of the North York Moors area. Sited on land slightly elevated above the River Rye, to be dry and safe from flooding, tranquil Harome boasts several beautiful, thatched cottages in an unspoilt sleepy setting.

An especially pretty stroll is along Ings Lane. This is the start of this walk and will take you past the ducks of the mill race to the picturesque stone-built Harome Mill. Opposite this are two fine examples of the English thatched cottage, including Mill Cottage itself.

The village green is lined by stone-built cottages which are, so far, happily free from the trappings of the tourism business. Harome is a gentle quiet backwater from which to base this equally gentle walk over the fields of the Rye.

The Walk

Beginning with your back to the Star, head right, along the street as far as the road junction by the church. Turn right along Ings Lane towards Harome Siding and continue past Harome Mill on your right and the last of the village's cruck-framed thatched cottages on your left until you arrive at a T-junction.

Turn right to cross a white-railed bridge over the stream and, ignoring a public footpath immediately on your left, walk straight down the lane past Aby Green Farm.

At the farm there is a divide in the ways. Press straight on, along what is now Hall Lane to pass the old railway cottages at Harome Siding. Rounding a corner to the left, you arrive quite suddenly at the end of the lane. Go through the wooden gate and walk along the bridleway to the left-hand edge of the pasture. At the field boundary, pass through a pair of waymarked wooden gates and continue straight on with the River Rye now on your right.

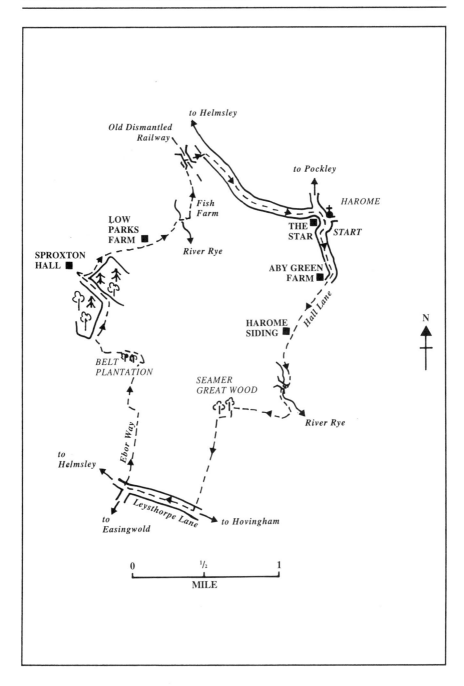

Walk along the right-hand edge of this field until you come to a footbridge crossing the river. On the other side, turn left and walk along the edge of the field with the river now on your left.

Follow the path around to the left and, through a gap in the hedge, into a grassy, uncultivated area where there are brambles. Keeping the river to your left, you will come to a place where there is a ford.

Turn right here, onto the track which leads across the field in front of you. Where the track splits, follow the waymarked footpath to the right, along the edge of a field, hedge to your left.

As you arrive at a wooded area on your left, part of Seamer Great Wood, you will find waymarking guiding you over a small metal footbridge. Walk around the woodland, keeping the trees always on your right, until you reach a waymarked stile in the corner of the field. Cross the stile and turn left, walking up the rise, with the hedge on your left, until, at the top corner of the second field, you reach a waymark post. This guides you in the same direction, along the edge of a third field, and then to a stile which you cross to reach Leysthorpe Lane.

Turn right alongside this B-road (the B1257) and walk up to its junction with the B1363. At this point a section of the Ebor Way long distance path leads off to the right. Follow this along West Newton Grange farm road. Where the farm road bends right you carry straight on, still following the Ebor Way, along the edge of the field with the hedgerow on your left. Reaching the field corner, just in front of Seamer Little Wood, the waymarking takes you left, and then right at the next corner.

Still walking alongside the hedge to your left, you will come to a wooden footbridge across White Beck. Cross the bridge and continue straight ahead when you reach the other side. Arriving at the trees of Belt Plantation, turn right and then left to skirt its edge, passing through a gate and turning left again to make your way along the back of the plantation.

Continue along the edge of a pasture, through a single gate and on to the far corner of the next field where there is a wooden signpost. Turn right, still along the Ebor Way, and follow the hedgerow up the field.

Going through a single wooden gate, continue around the field edge to a further gate bringing you onto a farm track. Turn left through the larger metal gate and walk along through the trees until you see Sproxton Hall ahead.

Just before you reach Sproxton Hall you arrive at a junction of trackways. Turn right here, almost back on yourself, and walk towards the trees. Keep following the track as it dips down into the woods and rises again to more open land.

At the point where the track takes a decided left turn to enter Low Parks Farm, you need to carry straight on along the grass track in front of you. Cross the waymarked stile you reach and walk along the edge of the pasture, wire fence to your right, towards the trees.

Ignore the gate leading right into the trees, but follow the fence until you join a track leading down from Low Parks Farm. Follow this diagonally down to the left to a waymark arrow in the bottom corner of the field. This leads you down to a second gate where there is a waymarked stile to cross. Carry on along the edge of the next field, hedge on your left, to a gate which you should pass through before bearing right down the grassy slope, alongside the hedgerow to a further gate.

On the other side of the gate you will be walking alongside an area of water to your right. This is not actually the River Rye, but a cut-off loop abandoned by it as its meandering course has changed over the years. There are several such loops, or ox-bow lakes as they are sometimes called, along this gentle section of the Rye, and you may have noticed another example by the footbridge just south of Harome Siding.

Walk alongside the wire fence, past a stile, to a metal gate. Go through the gate and walk around the edge of the pasture to the footbridge which you can see directly opposite you. This takes you over the River Rye to a fish farm. Turn left along the grassy track until it joins the main track which serves the fish farm. Follow this through a waymarked gate to a right-hand bend.

Instead of following the main track up to the right, carry straight on. There is a stile to help you across the low wire fence. Ignore the path which dips leftward to the river and has a handrail. Keep straight on.

There is a drainage ditch to your right, and the path soon takes you over a sluice for this before bringing you to a waymarked gate. Through the gate, follow the path straight ahead, along the bottom edge of the pasture with the wire fence and river to your left.

A waymark sign on a fence post guides you slightly right as the trodden path deviates slightly from the fence-line, taking you across the pasture to the old railway embankment. There is a stone bridge here where the railway used to cross a lane.

Turn right, negotiate the metal gate, and pass under the disused railway by means of this stone archway. Walk up the right-hand edge of the pasture field you find on the other side.

At the top corner of the field, you will come, through a gate where there is a public bridleway sign, to a minor road. Turn right and walk alongside the road towards Harome and the Star.

The Star

Walk 23: Roseberry Topping and Captain Cook's Monument

Route: Newton under Roseberry – Roseberry Topping – Great Ayton Moor – Captain Cook's Monument – Southbrook Farm – Cliff Ridge Wood – Newton Wood – Newton under Roseberry

Distance: $6^1/_2$ miles

Map: O.S. Outdoor Leisure 26, North York Moors Western Area (NW Sheet)

Start: The King's Head, Newton under Roseberry (Grid reference 571130)

Access: Newton under Roseberry is on the A173 Stokesley to Guisborough road, $1^1/_2$ miles north east of Great Ayton. The Tees 281 bus, from Stokesley, Guisborough and Redcar calls at the village and operates 7 days a week. The bus stop is directly opposite the King's Head.

The King's Head (0642 722318)

Dating back to 1796, this real ale house lies at the foot of "Cleveland's Matterhorn" – Roseberry Topping. Famous in the past for its own draught porter, it nowadays serves hand-pulled John Smiths Magnet and is open 11.30am to 3.00pm and 6.30pm to 11pm, Mondays to Saturdays. Sunday opening is 12 noon to 3pm and 7pm to 10.30pm. Bar and à la carte meals are served every session, and four-course lunch on Sunday.

Roseberry Topping

Approximately 1050 feet above sea level, capped by resistant gritstone, this curious hill represents a climb of just over 700 feet from Newton under Roseberry. The Topping (meaning a conical hill) was sacred to the Norse god Odin and was once known as Othensburg (Hill of Odin). The name Newton under Othensburg may have been corrupted to become Newton under Roseberry.

Ironstone, jet and alum have been mined here. Such workings are likely to have combined with natural slope wasting processes to cause the collapse of the upper part of the hill in 1912 and so create the present unusual profile of the Topping.

Roseberry Topping

Captain Cook's Monument

This stone obelisk was originally erected on 1064 feet high Easby Moor, in 1827, and restored in 1895, to celebrate local hero Captain James Cook. He was born in Marton in 1728, spent much of his youth in Easby and was educated in Great Ayton, before circumnavigating the globe, only to be killed in Hawaii in 1779.

The Walk

From the King's Head, turn left along the road through the village as far as the end of the cottages and then left again up Roseberry Lane – the track just before the public car park.

Continue through the wooden gates along the lane, and through the kissing gate into the woods. These are National Trust owned, and just to the left you will see an information display about Roseberry Common.

From this display board, head left to find a relatively gentle stone-laid path up towards the summit. This path ascends until it becomes a series of cut, wood-edged steps which take you around leftward onto a further section of stone path to a wooden gate.

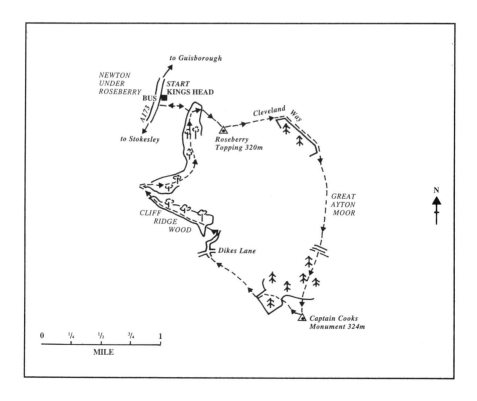

Beyond the gate, follow the obvious pathway straight ahead. Initially stone, this soon becomes a worn clay path. Press straight on, up towards the summit. Just before the summit itself the path leads you over a few rocks.

From the triangulation pillar, steel posts, set in the summit rock, point the way down, along the narrow ridge behind Roseberry Topping. On the descent you will find a wire fence to your right. At the base of the slope, make your way across to the point where this fence becomes dry stone wall.

Follow this wall, on your right, along what is now the Cleveland Way, until you begin to climb again as you pass a solitary tree. Pass a plantation on your right, following the path right, and around the back of the plantation, to a single wooden gate set in a dry stone wall. Pass through the gate and carry straight on, keeping the dry stone wall on your right. Continue to follow this wall across the moor, with open heather on your left.

As you pass alongside a second plantation, the wall peters out and becomes a wire fence. Follow the path straight down to the car park at the bottom of the slope. Reaching the minor road at the car park, turn right and walk along to wooden gates on the left. Follow the Cleveland Way through these gates and along the track into the Cleveland Forest.

At the top of the forest, the path up to Captain Cook's Monument continues straight ahead. From the Monument, turn obliquely right towards a pair of gate posts. Pass through these and straight along the path until a waymark arrow directs you left towards a conifer plantation.

The path takes you through the trees until it divides in two. Take the left-hand, main, fork downhill to reach a track crossing your route. Carry straight on down to a single wooden gate with waymark arrow.

Passing through the gate, wire fence and dry stone wall on your right, you will come to a corner in the dry stone wall. Turn right onto the track you find here and walk along until you reach a single wooden gate set in a dry stone wall. Through this gate you emerge onto a green lane between wire fenced pastures. Carrying on between hedgerows you will pass a large brick villa on your left, beyond which the lane is surfaced.

Coming to a crossroads, Dikes Lane heading up to the right, carry straight on and down Airey Holme Lane. Following this lane, it bends round to the right and passes a couple of white houses on your right. Beyond these, you reach some trees and a public footpath signposted leftward. Take this left turn and cross a waymarked wooden stile into a pasture field. Walk alongside the wire fence on your left and cross the next stile into deciduous woodland.

Follow the clear path straight ahead into the trees. Coming to another path crossing the route by an old metal kissing gate, stroll straight ahead through Cliff Ridge Wood. When the path emerges from the woods onto more open ground, carry straight on along the now gravel track. Where the track bends 90 degrees to the left, there is a path on your right.

The King's Head, Newton under Roseberry

Follow the path into trees, a fence to your left, and up to the National Trust sign. Take the left fork here, and walk along through the trees with the fence-line to your left again.

Stick to the main path through Newton Wood, ignoring any minor off-shoots, until, at a distinct fork, the main path appears to head right and uphill. Here you need to take the downhill, apparently minor, left fork. There is a boulder by this fork, and the path divides either side of an oak tree.

The left fork brings you down to the northern edge of the woodland, and the path initially follows the line of the wire fence. Keeping on this path, you will emerge into a clearing where the main path which you need to follow keeps low and bears to the left. The path then forks again. Stick to the policy of following the left hand, bottom, path and you will return to the southern end of Roseberry Lane.

Turning left onto the lane, follow it back into Newton under Roseberry.

Walk 24: Ingleby Greenhow

Route: Ingleby Greenhow – Bank Foot – Incline Top – Bloworth Crossing – Cleveland Way – Ingleby Bank – Bank Foot – Stone Stoup Hill – Ingleby Greenhow

Distance: 9 miles

Map: O.S. Outdoor Leisure 26, North York Moors Western Area (NW Sheet)

Start: The Dudley Arms (Grid reference 582064)

Access: Ingleby Greenhow is $2^1/_2$ miles east of Great Broughton, which lies on the B1257 Stokesley to Helmsley road, 2 miles south east of Stokesley. By bus, you can reach Ingleby Greenhow village from Stokesley on the Tees service 293, Mondays to Saturdays.

The Dudley Arms (0642 722526)

The Dudley is a stone-built 17th century coaching inn with a fine local reputation for food. The evening à la carte menu adds to the range of bar meals and sandwiches which are also offered at lunch-time. Real ale is Theakstons, and the Dudley Arms is open from 11am to 3pm and 7pm to 11pm Mondays to Fridays (an hour earlier on Saturday evenings) and the usual 12 noon to 3pm and 7pm to 10.30pm on Sunday.

Ingleby Greenhow

There are various Inglebies along the foot of the Cleveland Hills – Ingleby Cross and Ingleby Arncliffe lie a few miles to the west where the scarp ends and the Hambleton Hills begin. There is also Ingelby Barwick, a growing suburb of Teesside. Ingleby Greenhow is, however, a small village centred on an attractive classical terrace, capped by a triangular edifice including village clock, and encompassing a butcher's shop and the Post Office, as well as the pub, within it.

The village is situated at the northern end of its own green embayment of the Moors scarp and acts as the service centre for the several farms sheltering there.

The Incline

Visible from miles to the north, the Incline (it deserves its capital letter) is a steady, dead straight and remorseless pull up the northern flank of the North York Moors. A mile long, it originated in the heat of the Industrial Revolution as part of the railway built to bring Rosedale iron ore down from the Moors. The ore fed the iron and steel furnaces of the 'boom town' of Middlesbrough. In that mile, the Incline gains over 200m of height and wagons had to be hauled up the gradient using steel ropes – the remains of the winding house are still to be seen at the top.

The Walk

Beginning with your back to the Dudley Arms, turn right and walk along the road through the village, straight ahead at the junction, in the direction of Battersby Junction. The footpath you want is a cut between two houses on the right and is indicated by a public footpath sign.

Follow the narrow path between wood fences to a waymarked stile and cross into a field, following the path along the left-hand edge. At a second stile, cross into a succeeding field following the wire fence on your left.

Walking down to a third stile, cross it and continue along with the hedgerow on your right. A pair of waymark posts along here direct you straight ahead, until a third guides you left to a pasture field. Follow the wire fence along the left-hand edge of this field until you come to a waymarked stile. Instead of crossing this stile, turn right and walk along the field edge with the fence on your left.

Cross the next waymarked stile into an area of scrub and bear left to follow the line of the bramble-covered dry stone wall which is a few yards over to your left. Weaving between a number of small trees, you arrive at a grass track.

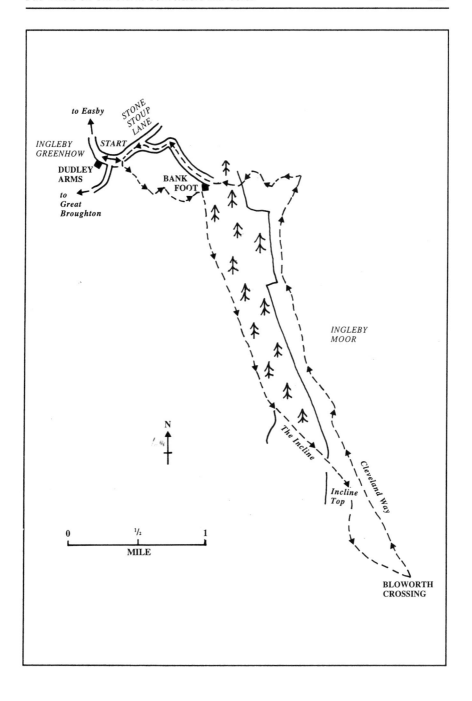

Turn left onto this track and follow it along, towards the buildings of Bank Foot, until you come to a metal gate. Head right here, along the lane you have now encountered.

Continue along this lane, passing a waymarked public footpath to your right, and a row of brick-built cottages on your left, and a second footpath off to the right, until you reach a wooden gate at the lane end.

Go through the gate and keep walking straight ahead, into the forest. At a divide in the ways, take the left-hand fork upward – the beginning of the Incline. Pass another waymarked footpath on your right. Just over half-way up the straight incline you cross a stile, but otherwise it is a simply a matter of heading straight on up to the top.

Achieving the Incline Top, carry straight on, following the line of the old railway. This takes you around to the right, before beginning a long sweep left through a low cutting and bringing you to the first of two gates across the way.

Beyond the first gate is a wooden bench beside a boundary stone for the Nawton Tower Estate. Then a track crosses your way from right to left. Turn left along it; it is the Cleveland Way.

Keep walking along this track. Along the way you will pass a tall boundary stone inscribed "F 1838", and beyond it a series of grouse butts. Keep on going until there is a divide in the track where the Cleveland Way signpost directs you along the right-hand fork via a green metal gate.

After the path has curved right, dipped down and then bent left, you will see a low cairn on your left where a track crosses from right to left. Turn left by this cairn, and the narrowing path will bring you down to a second cairn which is waymarked. Carry straight on and cross a little plank bridge before bearing right and coming upon a much wider stoney track.

Join this wider track and head downhill along it and around the bend to the left. This brings you down to a wooden gate at the woodland edge.

There is a footpath down through the trees from here, but you will have to have your eyes peeled to find it. Easier, perhaps, to follow the lane along and then down as it swings leftward.

Either way, you will arrive at a gate beside the buildings of Bank Foot. Pass through the gate and head straight on down the lane all the way to the minor road of Stone Stoup Hill where you turn left.

Walk along the road and back into Ingleby Greenhow and the Dudley Arms.

Walk 25: Carlton in Cleveland

Route: Carlton – Underhill House – Plane Tree Farm – Little Bonny Cliff – Gold Hill – Carlton Bank – Alum House Lane – Carlton.

Distance: 6 miles

Map: O.S. Outdoor Leisure 26, North York Moors Western Area (NW Sheet)

Start: The Blackwell Ox (Grid reference 508044)

Access: By bus Tees service 90/90A from Northallerton, Stokesley and Middlesbrough serves the village from Monday to Saturday.

If you are driving, you will find Carlton just half a mile south of the A172 Stokesley to Thirsk road, turning off as signposted, $2^1/_2$ miles west of Stokesley.

The Blackwell Ox (0642 712287)

The unusual and modern facade of the Blackwell Ox belies the much more traditional atmosphere of its cosy main bar where Bass and Worthington Best Bitter real ales are sold. Cheerfully busy in the evenings, the Blackwell Ox serves its village as a local, as well as attracting customers from the surrounding area.

Bar meals are served lunch-times and evenings, as is Sunday lunch. Unexpectedly, traditional Thai dishes are a speciality and are served every day except Tuesday.

There is a beer garden overlooking the green of this award winning village, and a chidren's play area.

Carlton in Cleveland

Carlton in Cleveland

A paradox is that 'Carlton in Cleveland' is not in Cleveland. It is in North Yorkshire.

That much is true if Cleveland is taken to mean the administrative county of that name. However, the name is older than any local government re-organisation; it can be taken to refer to the physical region of the Cleveland Hills and the lowlands between that northern scarp face of the North York Moors and the River Tees. In that sense Carlton is in Cleveland, and that is what its name suggests.

At any event, Carlton is a picture postcard village, Dalesman Best Village Award winner for 1981 and 1990, set at the foot of the forested Carlton Bank, on top of which a gliding club's aerodrome is somehow incongruously sited. Clearly the top of steep banks is good for lift, but it still makes for an odd sight as you walk along the Cleveland Way on the moor edge.

The Blackwell Ox

The Walk

Coming down the path from the Blackwell Ox, turn left along the road through Carlton, keeping the stream on your right until you reach the road junction. Go right, in the direction of Faceby, until you reach a public footpath sign on your left.

Cross the stile into a pasture and walk straight over to the far corner and cross the stile there into the next field, keeping the wire fence on your left. Carry on in this way over the fields and a series of stiles until you reach an ash track crossing your way from left to right.

Here a waymarked stile leads you onto a stony track. Follow the line of the wooden fence on your right until you cross a stream to a wooden gate where there is a stile to cross. Follow the track ahead of you across the middle of a grass field.

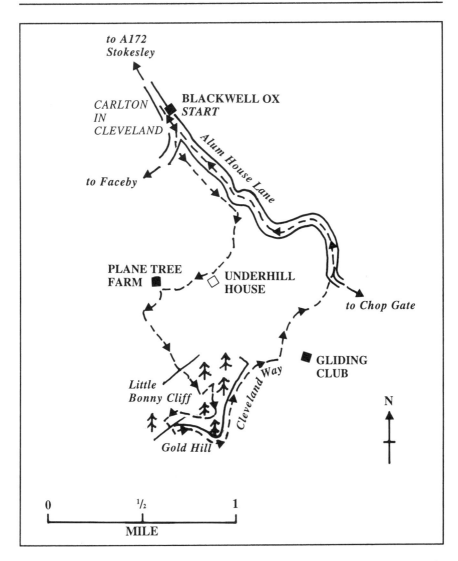

At the far boundary you will find a footpath sign directing you left. Ignore this and press straight on to a public footpath sign mounted on a tree at the field boundary.

Cross the stile here into another pasture and turn right to the corner of the field where you head left, keeping the wire fence on your right. Keep going across the fields to a wooden stile, and cross that to carry straight on initially, before curving right along the grass track, towards some farm buildings.

You are now at Plane Tree Farm. Checking with your O.S. map you may well notice that there has been some diverting of the footpaths in this area. Go through the gate at the end of the track and turn left along the lane to a point where there are three gates together.

Choose the right-hand gate and pass through to walk across the field with the hedge on your left. Coming to a junction of trackways, turn left to a gate and cross the stream, carrying straight on along the track.

Arriving at two gates, you should pass through the one on the left and head towards a ruin. Follow the track straight ahead to a stile. Cross this and continue until you reach a T-junction by a pond.

Just offset to the right is a path up through the trees. Follow this path as it curves up to the main track running through the forest. Turn right onto this until you fine a dry stone wall running up and down the slope.

Turn left and follow the wall uphill. This will bring you to the top of the trees by a big boulder. Just to the left is a step up and over the wall. Walk along to the left along the dry stone wall to a corner where there is a choice of pathways.

Choose the one which takes you straight on and brings you onto the Cleveland Way. Turn left and follow the Cleveland Way past the Gliding Club at the top of Carlton Bank to the triangulation pillar and then straight ahead and down to some stone steps and a waymarker post.

Coming to the bottom of the waymarked Cleveland Way descent, walk along a trackway to the left onto the surface minor road. Follow this downhill to a public footpath sign on the right which guides you down a grass path, with a fence on your right, until you re-join the road.

Carry on downhill, alongside the minor road, until you come back into Carlton and straight on to the Blackwell Ox.

Walk 26: Hawnby

Route: Hawnby – Church Bridge – Nags Head Wood – Arden Hall – Harker Gates – Half Moon Plantation – Carr House – Manor Farm – Hawnby

Distance: 5 miles

Map: O.S. Outdoor Leisure 26, North York Moors Western Area (SW Sheet)

Start: Hawnby Hotel (Grid reference 543898)

Access: Hawnby is in the upper reaches of Ryedale $3^1/_2$ miles north west of the B1257 Helmsley to Stokesley road, turning off 4 miles north of Helmsley. If driving from the north, the shortest route is to take the Laskill turning at the southern end of Bilsdale.

Hawnby Hotel (043 96 202)

The hotel is sited at the top of the hill, turn right there to find it and its car park just beyond. A stone-built building, its public bar is reached directly from the roadside and projects an urbane and civilised image when you enter the door.

Ahead is the bar counter itself on which is mounted the real ale pump dispensing John Smith's beneath a wooden ceiling. To the right just the one drinking table and to the left most of the tables, set out for eating. Around the walls is a shelf on which a collection of mostly ceramic owls stands sagely.

The floor is carpeted throughout and the design of this, and the wallpaper, is light and modern – different for a pub, even if it is a hotel's bar, but it works. The decor helps create a haven of peace and tranquillity, and, relaxing over a steak and ale pie, it is difficult not to have a sense of well-being and contentment.

Bar meals, including an "all day" breakfast, are served during the bar's opening hours of 11am to 3pm and 7pm to 11pm, except Sunday, when there is no alcohol served until noon.

Given the carpeting, it is a good idea not to plunge through the door in heavy, muddy boots – leave them in the car or, as others do, by the door.

The Hawnby Hotel

Hawnby

The picturesque little village of Hawnby is sited on an unusually steep hillside above the waters of the Rye. Consequently, its buildings and services are clustered in two groups – the Post Office amid the clump of habitation at the slope foot and the Hawnby Hotel 500 yards away at the hill top.

John Wesley preached here in the 18th century, having travelled over the Moors from Osmotherley (Walk 19), and the absence of a straightforward village pub may be related to the village's strong Methodist tradition. There is, however, an admittedly plainly simple, Norman church, of 12th century vintage, by the river.

The Walk

Coming out of the Hawnby Hotel, turn left and set off along the road until you come down to, and over, the stone Church Bridge. Crossing the River Rye, the public bridleway turns off very sharply to the left, indicated by a signpost.

Pass through the wooden gate and, for the first few yards, follow the wire fence on your left. However, as this fence bears left, you should

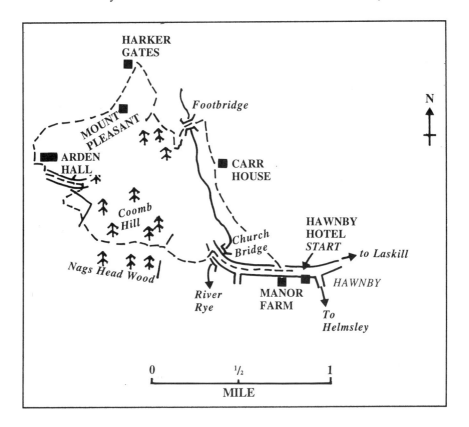

press straight on, slightly rightward, and uphill along the grass path towards a single large oak tree in the middle of the field.

Reaching the tree, you will see the track clearly, straight ahead of you. Passing a telegraph pole, you enter some trees and find a waymarked stile next to a gate. Follow the grass track up the rise beyond this stile, and pass through the next gate into a pasture field.

Turn right and walk up the edge of the field to the corner where you turn left and walk along the top edge to a waymarked hurdle gate.

Carrying straight on, the path brings you into Nags Head Wood and leads you straightforwardly through to the other side. Here you find another gate which is waymarked to guide you down diagonally to your left across the pasture. This gate is beside what little remains of the ruined Coomb House.

Reaching the track at the bottom of the slope, turn right along it, and proceed almost as far as the gate. A few yards in front of the gate, the path takes you right with rougher ground on your left dipping down to a spring.

The path then curves gently left and re-enters the woodland via a wooden gate. Walk down through the woods to the minor road. Turn left onto this road and walk along until it peters out and becomes a track. At this point, turn right as indicated by the bridleway signpost, and pass through the gateway of Arden Hall.

Walk down the driveway and then follow the waymarking to the left of the Hall, passing a barn and row of estate workers' houses on your right, before following the way right along the back of these cottages.

Follow the waymarking and come down into the woods. Here there is a seat in memory of members of a South Bank (Middlesbrough) rambling club – the St Peter's Rambling Association.

Meeting a second track, crossing the way from left to right, turn right along it and through the gate in front of you. Cross the field alongside the wire fence, and then hedgerow, to your right. Pass through the ungated gap into the next field and, finally, though a wooden gate onto another trackway. Turn left towards Mount Pleasant Farm.

Reaching the cattle grid at Mount Pleasant Farm, bear left towards a waymarked gate. Continue through this and across a pasture field by means of the track along the bottom edge. Pass through a second gate and carry on along the lane, just past the stone built cottage at Harker Gates.

Look carefully for the waymarked stile on your right which will take you over the wire fence into a pasture field and down to the right to the stream. Reaching the stream, follow it down a little to the wooden waymarked gate. Pass through this and bear left so that you cross the field to the stile in the opposite corner.

Crossing the stile, turn right along the track, crossing the cattle grid as you bend left. When the track comes to a very sharp right-hand bend, you press straight ahead, over a stile and along the side of a pasture field.

A wooden gate leads you onto a lane and so to Half Moon Plantation. Keep bearing left here and follow the track down hill along the edge of the trees. Reaching a ford, cross the stream and turn immediately left, through the wooden gate set in the dry stone wall, onto the stream bank. The stream is now on your left.

Cross the footbridge you see ahead of you and walk straight forwards between two rows of trees with the stream now on your right. The path then bends left to a single wooden gate. Through the gate, the track leads straight on, River Rye to the right. Following the track around a gentle right-hand bend, you will see a tubular steel footbridge among the riverside trees.

Use this footbridge to cross the river into Low Wood. Turn left, and follow the path as it bends around on itself to the right and begins to head uphill a little. Where you join another path, head left along the more clearly trodden way.

At the edge of the woodland, take the path to your right which leads you back into the woods. Follow the clear path to the end of the woodland. Emerging via a wooden gate, you will see ahead of you, and curving right towards a telegraph pole, a grass track. However, the path you want bears left at the point where the track curves rightward, and takes you uphill a little further to the brow of the pasture field.

From the brow, head straight on, so that you pass the buildings of Carr House on your left. From the edge of Carr House's enclosed garden, you can see the track wending its way down across the field, between two standing trees.

Follow this grass track to the two trees. On reaching them, bear left, leaving the line of the main track, and straight across to the waymarked wooden gate ahead of you.

Go through the gate and carry straight on towards the corner of the trees. Continue, keeping the fence and trees to your right, until, at the end of the woodland, you can see a wooden gate ahead of you.

This gate brings you onto a track which in turn leads through a farm gate and down to the minor road at Manor Farm. Turn left and walk back into Hawnby village, to the Hotel.

Walk 27: Ampleforth

Route: Ampleforth – Westwood Lane – Drakendale Gill – College Moor – High Street – Studford Ring – South View Farm – Ampleforth

Distance: $4^1/_2$ miles

Map: O.S. Outdoor Leisure 26, North York Moors Western Area (SW Sheet)

Start: The White Horse (Grid reference 581787)

Access: Ampleforth lies 2 miles south of the A170 road from Thirsk to Helmsley. By public transport, the village is reachable by locally operated Stephenson's Coaches of Easingwold (0342 21707) from Helmsley and York on Mondays to Saturdays.

The White Horse (04393 378)

This 17th century establishment is still an authentic village pub with a warm and friendly welcome. The pew-style benches of aged wood around the walls of the bar-room combine with the rest of the decor to create a traditional atmosphere untrammelled by indiscriminate modernisation.

It's open from 11am to 11pm on Saturdays and Bank Holidays, from 11am to 2.30pm and 6pm to 11pm Mondays to Fridays, with usual Sunday opening hours. The White Horse serves Tetley Bitter and John Smiths, to wash down a choice of bar meals and sandwiches available seven days a week, lunchtimes and evenings. Customers who are eating are given the option of doing so in the separate dining room if they prefer that to the bar itself.

Ampleforth

This delightful, stone-built linear village is most famous for its renowned Roman Catholic Abbey and Public School, $^3/_4$ mile east of the village on the road to Oswaldkirk. The monastery buildings are a mixture of styles and dates, but the oldest dates back to 1860. This is not, then, an ancient foundation, and it traces its origin back to the arrival of three French Benedictines at the dawn of the 19th century. The impressive Abbey Church itself is open to the public.

However, the village of Ampleforth is refreshingly little-affected by the presence of this institution. It remains an attractive, living, working village which well repays a stroll along its single street. My choice of the White Horse pub reflects this air of a genuine and surprisingly un-touristy village – you feel that the locals drink there.

Ampleforth College

The Walk

Leaving the White Horse, turn right and walk along the village main street until you cross the stream. Ignoring the public footpath signposted off to the right, carry straight along the road up the rise.

At the top of the rise a minor road leads off to the right in the direction of Hambleton. Pass this by, and carry on to the next right turn, by a No Through Road sign. Turn right up this lane, Westwood Lane, and follow it up and around to the left passing the saw mill on the right and a stone cottage on your left.

Keep following the lane between the hedgerows until you come to a gate across the way. Pass through the gate and, initially, continue along the

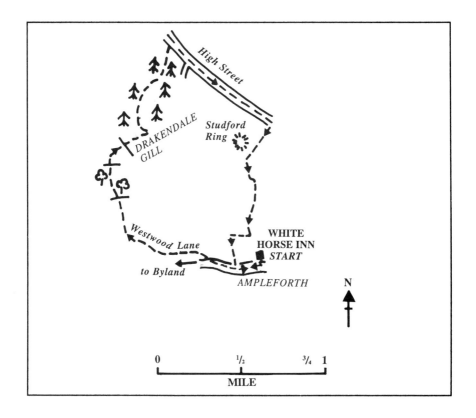

track as it swings right and then comes to a left-hand, hair-pin bend. Instead of following the track around this second sharp bend, carry on in a straight line, initially alongside a wire fence on your right, the stream to your left.

Cross the stile you reach, into the woods, following the clearly trodden, main path straight through the woods. Passing a waymarked tree, you will come, after a little climb up a gulley, to a distinct T-junction of woodland pathways. Turn left here. Following the way round, you will begin to see another track on the opposite bank of a gill. This track and the one you are following then join, and, when they do so, you should bear right along the resulting lane.

This will bring you up to the minor road. Turn right and follow the road past the road junction and onto High Street. Pass Studford Farm on your right and then take the public footpath which is indicated on your right.

Cross the stile onto a grass trackway which you follow straight ahead, passing the ancient earthwork of Studford Ring on your right, until a waymark arrow directs you left over a stile. Walk along the edge of the field in which you now find yourself, keeping the hedge on your right. At the corner of this first field the path bends slightly right to take you along the edge of a second field. Again, you are following a hedgerow on your right.

At the corner of this second field, a waymark arrow leads you left and along the field edge with the hedge still to your right and a wire fence now to your left. This brings you to a metal farm gate which you do not pass through. Instead, you will now see on your right a waymarked stile leading into a pasture field.

Walk along the edge of this field, wire fence and dry stone wall on your left. At the bottom corner of this field is a gate which you should pass through and continue along with fence and wall still on your right.

The next target is a gate halfway along the next field boundary, rather than in the actual corner. Across this gate is a new wooden fence line which you should follow to a stable block. Follow the track straight down through two gates in succession.